LOOKING FOR HIM IN ALL OF THEM

Simone Alysha Cassell

SCRIBES & SCEPTER PUBLISHERS

Looking For Him In All of Them

Copyright © 2025 Simone Alysha Cassell.

Published in Queensland, Australia by Scribes & Scepter Publishers.

Scribes & Scepter titles are available for bulk purchase for educational, ministry, business, fundraising, or promotional use. To inquire about bulk orders, please contact us at simone@simonecassell.com.

All rights reserved. No part of this publication may be copied, stored in a retrieval system, or shared in any form whether electronic, mechanical, photocopied, recorded, or otherwise without written permission from the publisher. Exceptions apply for brief quotations used in reviews, articles, or scholarly works, provided they are properly cited.

Scripture quotations marked (NLT) are from the New Living Translation, copyright © 1996, 2004, 2015 by Tyndale House Foundation. Used by permission of Tyndale House Publishers, Inc., Carol Stream, Illinois 60188. All rights reserved.

Scripture quotations marked (TPT) are from The Passion Translation. Copyright © 2017, 2018, 2020 by Passion & Fire Ministries, Inc. Used by permission. All rights reserved.

Scripture quotations marked (KJV) are from the King James Version of the Bible. Public domain.

Scripture quotations marked (NIV) are from the Holy Bible, New International Version®, NIV®. Copyright © 1973, 1978, 1984, 2011 by Biblica, Inc.™ Used by permission of Zondervan. All rights reserved worldwide.

Cover design by Scribes & Scepter Publishers
Interior design and layout by Scribes & Scepter Publishers

First Edition

Ebook ISBN: 978-1-7641021-0-0
Paperback ISBN: 978-1-7641021-1-7

For more information visit: www.simonecassell.com

Disclaimer

The content of this book reflects the personal experiences, reflections and perspectives of the author. It is intended to inspire and encourage, but is not a substitute for professional, medical, therapeutic, clinical or pastoral advice. We encourage readers facing emotional or mental health challenges to seek support from qualified professionals.

All brand names, including Reebok® are used for identification purposes only and are property of their respective owners. This book is not affiliated with or endorsed by Reebok. Reebok® is a registered trademark of its respective owner.

This work includes references to the publicly reported case of Gabby Petito, whose life and legacy deeply impacted the author. With the utmost respect and compassion, the Author shares these reflections to honour her memory and bring light, awareness, and healing to others who may be navigating silent battles. All references to public figures or real-life events are included for commentary or educational purposes only, and no affiliation or endorsement is implied. The section honouring Gabby Petito reflects the author's personal experience and is not intended to represent or speak on behalf of the Petito family.

This book is a work of non-fiction. To protect privacy, the Author has altered names and identifying details of individuals.

To the ones who still dare to hope—this is for you.

To my younger self—you were never broken, only becoming.

To the One who restores all things and brings beauty from ashes—my anchor, my healer, my hope.

AUTHOR'S NOTE

If you're holding this book, it's not by accident. I pray these pages stir up hope where it's been lost, ignite healing where pain has lingered, remind you there's still purpose in your story—and draw your heart closer to the One who will never let go.

With love,
Simone Alysha Cassell

Download the **FREE *7-Day Reflection & Journal Companion*** that accompanies this book. Designed to help you unpack what you've read and guide you through your own healing journey.

www.simonecassell.com/resources

TABLE OF CONTENTS

Preface 1

Part 1: The Search
Chapter 1: Once Upon a Boy 5
Chapter 2: Looking for Love (Everywhere but Up) 14
Chapter 3: Red Flags and Rose-Coloured Glasses 24

Part 2: The Breaking Point
Chapter 4: The Fixer Trap:
    When Helping Becomes Hiding 41
Chapter 5: Rock Bottom and Reeboks® 48
Chapter 6: The Breaking Before the Breakthrough 64

Part 3: The Breakthrough
Chapter 7: The Love I Never Knew 75
Chapter 8: Healing the Girl in the Mirror 85
Chapter 9: Looking for Him in All of Them
    (and Finally Finding Him) 96

About the Author 115

PREFACE

Before We Begin

I didn't set out to write a book.

I set out to heal.

To make sense of the patterns, the pain, and the parts of myself I kept losing in the name of love. To finally step out of the cycle and step into something real, something whole.

It's not a record of wrongs, it's a record of revelation. It's about pausing long enough to ask honest questions: Where did I lose myself? Why did I keep settling? And what was I truly looking for?

Maybe you've asked those questions too.

Maybe you've loved deeply and lost yourself.

Maybe you've stayed too long, shrunk too small, or carried a version of yourself you no longer recognise.

If that's you, you're not alone. This book is for you.

Looking for Him in all of them is not about blaming men, romanticising pain, or offering step-by-step healing formulas. It's about getting honest. Letting go of love that breaks you, so you can receive the love that heals you. The love of the One who loved you first.

SIMONE ALYSHA CASSELL

This isn't a highlight reel. It's a story of unravelling, rebuilding and rising.

And my prayer is that you don't just find peace in my story as you read these pages. That you also find a deep and lasting peace in your own journey—and the freedom and hope to write a new story of your own.

With love,
Simone Alysha Cassell

PART 1

THE SEARCH

"He heals the wounds of every shattered heart."
Psalm 147:3 (TPT)

CHAPTER 1

ONCE UPON A BOY

The Fairy Tale Script

I always thought I'd be married by twenty-four. Not because of some divine revelation or an unwavering childhood dream, but because that's just what you did. My mum did it. Her friends did it. The movies confirmed it. Somewhere between playing dress-ups and navigating teenage crushes, I absorbed the message loud and clear—your twenties were a countdown clock to love, marriage, and the happily ever-after.

And I believed it. Well, most of me did.

But deep, deep down—buried beneath the rom-coms, the bridal magazines and the well-meaning relatives who asked if I had a "special someone" yet, something inside me knew I wanted more. Not that I didn't want love or marriage, but I had this unshakable sense that my story was bigger. Like a compass inside me was being pulled in a different direction, but society had already programmed the GPS route. Find a man, fall in love, get married, have children. Mission accomplished.

So, naturally, I set off on that mission with the determination of a woman who had places to be and a timeline to stick to. I didn't question it. I had established the plan and it was right on cue.

The first boy I fell for in my late teens? Oh, he was everything I thought I wanted. Handsome, charming, made me laugh and, best of all, he fit the picture. He ticked every box. The way he made me feel "alive", like the butterflies, was a sign that I was on the right track. That this was it. The dream was unfolding before my eyes. I could already see it: the wedding invitations (simple but elegant), the house (white picket fence, obviously) and the life we'd build together. It was happening.

Except it wasn't.

Looking back, I should've seen the warning signs. But red flags often appear as endearing quirks, particularly to young, hopefuls conditioned to believe love is everything. He was emotionally unavailable? That just meant he was deep. He made me feel small? No, no, I just needed to try harder to make him happy. We had completely different values? Opposites attract, right?

Newsflash: They don't.

I disregarded my gut feelings and followed the assigned script. Whether that be society's script or the one in my mind, it was there. And the script, which said that if I just loved hard enough, waited long enough, and overlooked enough, it would all work out. Because that's what good women do. A man determines a woman's worth and they persevere through difficulties. They possess patience. Work at understanding. And they wait for love to show up.

The thing was, it wasn't love showing up. It was me, trying to love someone who couldn't love me back. I was trying to fit myself into someone else's mould. Trying to be what they needed me to be rather than stepping into who I truly was. And somewhere in all of that, I lost track of the one thing that could've set me free from it all. At least in the rational decision-making sense: Myself and my decisions.

It took years—more than I'd like to admit—to see how flawed the script had been. The love I longed for wasn't hiding in another person. A wedding dress and a new last name didn't contain the missing pieces of my identity. Perhaps all along the search for belonging had really been a search for Him. And that maybe, just maybe, I had been searching for Him in all of them.

But there I was, still convinced I'd found the right path. On the hunt. Still chasing. I was still trying to fit love into that perfect little box I'd been promised. The story that was supposed to be mine.

I was like a child who'd been told a fairytale and now I couldn't let go of it. I clung to the happily ever after, even though reality differed greatly from the story I'd bought into.

And so, the journey began.

Before the guy I'm about to tell you more about, there were crushes—those innocent crushes that seemed like the real thing back then. In high school I had convinced myself that I was in love a dozen times over. My heart would race when a certain boy smiled at me in class, or when he casually brushed past me in the hallway. In those fleeting moments I'd build entire futures in my mind—picking out the names of our kids, imagining the house we'd live in and planning the holidays. But none of those crushes amounted to much beyond the fantasy in my mind. They were the first drafts of love. Where I got to practice the art of dreaming up the fairytale.

And then came "him".

The first "real" boyfriend—let's call him the "love of my life". I met him around age 18-19. Everything seemed to fall into place (somewhat). He was the personification of what I thought love was supposed to look like: charming, funny, attractive (to me)—everything I wanted. We spent hours talking about everything under the sun, laughing until our stomachs hurt and dreaming up wild ideas for our future. We were inseparable, or at least I thought we were. I couldn't wait to plan our wedding (yes, already), and live happily ever-after. But beneath that surface was something I couldn't quite put my finger on. The cracks in the foundation were there, but they were small, insignificant, or so I convinced myself.

At first, the relationship was everything I had hoped for. But slowly, the cracks grew, and I found myself in a whirlwind of confusion. He was everything, yet somehow, he wasn't. One moment he was loving, the next he was cold. He was tender, but then, suddenly, cruel. I doubted myself, second-guessed everything I thought I knew about love. Was it me? Was I doing something wrong? I thought it was my job to fix things, to make him see the light, to make him happy. If I just loved him more, it would all work out. That was the story I'd been drip fed, after all. Love conquers all, right?

But love, I learned the hard way, doesn't conquer everything. At least, not that kind of "love". Let's be real—I had no clue what love really was, either to give or to receive. But the ideal of love? Oh, I knew that all too well.

In hindsight, it seems almost absurd how much I let myself get lost in someone else. I moved in with him (secretly)—against my better judgement, against the warnings of my friends and family, who could see the red flags from a mile away. But I was so far gone in the fairy tale, I didn't care about the flags. I was determined to make this work. So, I bought a dog—an adorable little puppy, thinking maybe, just maybe, this may help things "stick". Maybe if I stayed long enough, loved him hard enough, things would get better. Maybe it would all fall into place if I just tried harder.

But it didn't.

It was like living in a constant state of emotional whiplash. The arguments became frequent and intense. He'd lash out over the smallest things—things I could never quite understand. I'd apologise for things I didn't even do, bending over backwards to keep the peace. It wasn't just the shouting; it was the silence in between. The coldness. The isolation. When he was upset, his eyes conveyed I was the problem, solvable with more effort from me. But the more I tried to fix things, the worse they became.

And then, the physical violence. It started small—shoves, pushes, the occasional grab. I convinced myself that it wasn't abuse, that maybe I had provoked it. I brushed it off as "normal" for a relationship, a misguided attempt at passion, maybe. I had no idea what real love was supposed to look like. I didn't know what was healthy or what was toxic. So I ignored it until it became unavoidable.

I became a prisoner of my own confusion, locked in a battle between what I thought I wanted and the reality that was slowly suffocating me. The physical abuse escalated. It wasn't just about the shoves anymore; it was the complete disregard for my safety and dignity. But I stayed. I didn't know how to leave. I thought it was normal to want to be loved this badly, no matter what it cost me. I thought that this was what love looked like, or if it's not love, it's close enough. Then came the night I'll never forget.

SIMONE ALYSHA CASSELL

Foot First & Falling

With puppy underarm, I realised I was locked out. Locked out of the house, that is. I should've taken a deep breath, sucked up my pride, and just walked away. But nope, that was not the path I chose. In a rather twisted blend of fear, insecurity, and desperation, I decided that the glass - plate door needed to be kicked in—because, apparently, my foot was the best tool for the job. Forget the pot plant or the rocks in the garden. This was serious business.

And oh, was it serious! As my foot met the glass, the blood told a different story. A sharp sting at my ankle, followed by a rush of blood that poured down my leg as I hobbled up the driveway, puppy still clutched in my arms.

Now, I know what you're thinking: Why didn't I just call for help? Or maybe you've skipped straight to, 'Who is this emotionally chaotic woman and how did she survive this long unsupervised?' Well, in the middle of it all, I didn't have the luxury of thinking. I was too busy panicking. That's when I knocked—well, more like half-hopped, half-knocked on the door of the townhouse two doors up. In a block of just four townhouses, and with the neighbour I'd never met, well, I was about to meet him, and oh, was he in for a surprise?

Seconds felt like minutes as I stood there, blood dripping all over my neighbour's front porch, hoping someone would answer. And then—miracle of miracles—the door swung open, and there he was: the neighbour I'd never met before. Or, should I say, an angel in disguise? "Come in, I'm a doctor," he said. It was surreal. A man, who just happened to be a doctor, was standing in front of me, blood-soaked and all. The situation was getting more bizarre by the moment.

LOOKING FOR HIM IN ALL OF THEM

The rest is a little blurry, but I remember lying on his living room floor, blood still flowing like an overzealous faucet. One of the few small mercies: the flooring was tile, not carpet—a miracle in itself, really. And, as they say, the rest is history. He stopped the bleeding and saved my life. Turns out, I'd slashed a nerve, a tendon, and, quite obviously, an artery in my foot. Who knew that kicking in a door could be such a dramatic affair?

In that moment of physical and emotional pain, I don't think I realised how much more pain was ahead of me. It felt like everything had come crashing down. Truth was, that was only the beginning. I knew it was the end of that "relationship," and the warning alarms to get the heck out of there had never been louder. Any abuse I'd endured up to that point had been bad enough, but, ironically, it was my own emotional distress and self-inflicted desperation that could have taken my life that evening.

If only that had been the first and last lesson in toxic relationships. If only. But no, the journey was only just beginning.

I couldn't see it then, but in hindsight, I was being saved, piece by piece, even in the messiest of moments. Or maybe, as I like to call it now, I was being "unravelled." Each lesson and every poor relationship was leading me one step closer to the genuine revelation and love I had been seeking all along. But that comes later, much later.

Back to that present day...

And there I was, in a townhouse block of just four, and my neighbour—whom I'd never met before—just happened to be the exact person I needed at that moment. Not a charming prince. Not a knight in shining armour - better than that; A Doctor. If that wasn't the hand of God in action, I don't know what was.

I think about that night more often than I care to admit, not because of the blood, the hospital, or even the permanent scar that now marks my ankle. Nor the lingering reminder of nerve damage that left my right foot permanently numb—but because of what it came to represent. It was the breaking point. Literally and figuratively. That moment was the messy, dramatic exclamation mark on a season I had no business trying to endure to survive.

That relationship had hurt me before. But it was the first time, physically, I couldn't ignore it anymore. Pain has a way of speaking when we've silenced every other voice. And this pain? Oh, it screamed at me. It was as if God had finally intervened in a language I couldn't argue with: Blood and consequence.

The hospital visit was long and blurry. Laced with questions I didn't want to answer. "What happened?" "How did you get this injury?" I can't even recall what I actually said or if it was the truth. Because, at that point, the truth felt too heavy to carry. Even to speak it out loud would've made it real. And I wasn't ready for reality. Not yet.

I remember staring at the ceiling in that emergency room, a bandage wrapped tightly around my foot, feeling equal parts relieved to be alive and ashamed that it had come to this. I didn't want to be that girl. You know the one. The girl who stayed too long. The girl who ignored the signs. The girl who got hurt. But I was.

And maybe that's the part no one talks about—how easy it is to judge from the outside. To look at someone else's chaos and think, *well, I would never put up with that.* But when you're in the mess, when others have chipped away at your self-worth piece by piece. When someone has twisted love into something unrecognisable—it's not that simple. It's not that clear.

LOOKING FOR HIM IN ALL OF THEM

There were days I missed him, not because he was good to me, but because I had become addicted to the idea of him. The potential. The promises. The fantasy I had created in my head.

But fantasies don't build futures. It wasn't love, it was validation disguised as romance. People-pleasing, cloaked in codependency. Fear, dressed up in a wedding gown.

I didn't walk away from that relationship as a warrior. I crawled. Limped, really. And a scar—visible and deep—that would always remind me of the girl who survived.

I wish I could say that was the last time I ever got it wrong. After that, I magically chose only healthy relationships and that I saw all the red flags and ran fast in the other direction. But I didn't. There were many more lessons. Many more heartbreaks. Much more. Because real life doesn't wrap itself up neatly in chapters. Healing doesn't arrive on schedule.

So, if you're reading this, maybe with your own wounds, your own questions, your own messy story—I want you to know this: You're not alone. And whatever fairytale you've been told, whatever picture-perfect timeline you've been clinging to, whatever "love" you've been trying to force into the frame—there is more.

And the actual story? It's just the beginning.

> *"For I know the plans I have for you," declares the Lord, "plans to prosper you and not to harm you, plans to give you a hope and a future."*
> *Jeremiah 29:11*

CHAPTER 2

LOOKING FOR LOVE (EVERYWHERE BUT UP)

Love—or more specifically, 'the one', was supposed to be my salvation. At least, that's what I thought. Over the years, from teenage crushes to adult relationships, I carried that belief like gospel. If I could just find the right man, the one who would see me, choose me, love me enough to quiet the restlessness inside—then everything would fall into place. That was the fairy tale I had subscribed to and I kept flipping through the pages, hoping each new chapter would be the one where it finally all made sense. But it never delivered—and it never could.

Every relationship I entered followed the same script. Different leading man, same tragic plot line. It always started with the rush, the all-consuming intensity of the "new" guy. Someone found me fascinating and suddenly I existed in technicolor. My phone would light up with their name and my stomach would twist in that giddy, addictive way. It felt like proof I was on the right path and that "the one" just hadn't caught up with me yet. Like validation I hadn't even realised I was starving for. I wasn't just waiting for love—I was hunting it, moulding myself into whatever shape seemed most likely to make it stick.

And then, inevitably, the unravelling would begin. The high would wear off and I felt that old familiar ache. The one that whispered, 'This isn't enough. You're not enough'. But instead of recognising it as my own deep-seated wound, I'd redirect my focus. If I just tried harder, loved better, fixed him, then surely, the missing piece would click into place. Surely, this time would be different.

But it never was. Because the truth, the one thing I was determined not to see, was that I was playing the same role over and over, with a rotating cast of broken men. And me? I was the tireless, hopeful repairwoman. Believing that if I could just glue their shattered pieces back together, I would finally be whole too.

Even as a teenager, I had an awareness of God. I believed, I really did. There were moments when I could feel something bigger, something real. And I certainly always had faith. But God was quiet, invisible. Men, on the other hand, were tangible. They could look me in the eye, hold my hand. Tell me I was special. And so, somewhere along the way, I shelved God in favour of something I could touch.

It was a slow unravelling—one I didn't even notice happening. A gradual trade-off where I exchanged faith for the pursuit of love because love felt like the ultimate prize. The happily ever-after. The thing that would fill the aching void in my chest.

But at what cost?

How many times would I live out the same toxic story before realising I was stuck in an endless loop? Each man became a chapter in a book I wasn't really living. I had no control over the plot. No idea that I was merely recycling the same heartbreak in different packaging. And with each new chapter, another piece of my confidence and self-respect eroded. Every time my hopes rose, every time I thought—Maybe this one! Only to end up right back in the same place—disappointed, drained, and lonelier than before, my identity shattered just a little more.

Subconsciously, a message was forming: There is something deeply wrong with me. Why didn't this chapter ever play out the way I longed for? Why didn't my life deliver the fairy tale ending promised to me?

Almosts, Maybes and Misfires

Some men were unexpected additions to my story—like Mark, my friend. The safe one. The guy I never saw "that way"— until one day, I did. And suddenly, there it was: Maybe it's meant to be. Maybe the one I was looking for was right in front of me all along. The classic "just friends… until we weren't" storyline. You know the one, like in '*When Harry Met Sally*', but with more existential angst and way less witty banter. He was safe. Familiar. The guy who would always pick up the phone, always check in and always remind me that I deserved better—which was ironic, given that he wasn't actually offering better himself.

Mark was in the Navy, which meant he was gone a lot. When he was in town, I was number one: dinners, long talks, the simple comfort of knowing someone had my back. But then he'd vanish again, off to another country, another mission, and I'd be left stranded in a sea of insecurity.

I told myself we had something real, something rare. But in reality? I was just the girl waiting at the dock while he sailed off into the distance, leaving me with nothing but an overstuffed suitcase of emotional baggage and a playlist full of sad love songs. Let's be honest, there were likely a few other 'ports' along the way… eventually to be confirmed in what turned out to be a wildly bizarre love triangle I never signed up for. But I convinced myself that what we had was special. Surely, when he came back, it would all make sense.

After Mark, I still didn't get it.

Enter Corey.

Corey was everything I thought I wanted on the surface—dark hair, piercing eyes and an effortless confidence that turned heads. Confidence bordering on arrogance. He was exactly the guy I gravitated toward—bold, magnetic, the type who made other men seem smaller by comparison. The way he moved, the way he spoke, it all screamed: 'this is it'!

At first, it felt like a dream. The chemistry was undeniable. He was my type… and then some. But being my type didn't mean he was good for me. Passion and sparks didn't make something real. Corey was all fire, no foundation—the kind of man who keeps you spinning but never lands long enough to build anything lasting.

In the end, I still felt just as lost and unsure.

Then came Shane.

Classic case of mistaking intensity for depth. He was electric. Unpredictable. The guy who kept me on my toes and made it feel like we were starring in a romance novel that only we could understand.

Red flags? Plenty. But I'd already written him into my narrative. Surely this one. Surely I can fix this.

Shane had that intoxicating blend of chaos and charm that made him impossible to resist. Every conversation felt like a roller coaster. One minute, he was all in—whispering promises about the future—and the next, he'd pull away without warning, caught up in something he couldn't, or wouldn't explain.

And yet, when he was present, it felt like magic. The rest of the time, I was bracing for the next storm. I told myself it was passion. That our connection was deep. But the truth? It was just chaos masquerading as meaning.

Between these chapters was what I'd call the date boys—the supporting cast in my ongoing romantic drama. Men who came and went in the quieter moments, often fading into the background once their scene was over. Not because I didn't care, but because I was chasing something bigger. The fairytale ending.

Some were lovely. Some were just there for a good time. But none of them stuck. The truth was, I wasn't really sure what I was searching for. Maybe I was always searching for something I couldn't name. So I filled the spaces with half-hearted connections—temporary, surface-level, never quite enough to fill the void. But nothing ever felt permanent, nothing felt real, and none of them ever truly "fit" the fairytale.

Liam was walking charisma, just the right amount of charm, with his own unique brand of confusion. The type who made you question whether emotional unavailability was a prerequisite for being disarmingly attractive. He had that look—the kind that could make you miss your exit. I sent a screenshot to friends and got the classic: "Girl He's hot… but RUN." Naturally, I did not run. I strolled—leisurely—right into the next beautiful disaster.

LOOKING FOR HIM IN ALL OF THEM

He was the type to ask deep questions about life, then pull out his phone mid-conversation to check Instagram. He had a way of making you feel like the only woman in the world, until you actually needed something real. Then it was: Sorry, I've just got a lot going on and also, I might be texting someone else at the same time.

Liam wasn't all bad. We had fun. Vodka cruisers, spontaneous karaoke—those kinds of adventures. But emotionally, he was like a flickering Wi-Fi signal in a blackout. Beautiful to look at, impossible to connect with. He'd smile like he was all in, and you'd find yourself halfway to planning your wedding, until he went radio silent for 48 hours.

When he finally reached back out, he'd reply with something like, "Sorry, was at the gym," and then post a photo of his abs on social media like it was a public service announcement to his loyal admirers.

Liam wasn't completely shut off, though. Occasionally, he'd drop lines like, "Life's about balance"—right before vanishing off the face of the earth again for two weeks. His version of balance meant emotionally ghosting and leaving me to overthink everything.

I learned that Liam's idea of "connection" was more about creating tension than it was about actually understanding each other. It's like a Netflix show you watch but never really care about the ending—except with Liam, I was the one who was left hanging at the season finale, with no closure. Looking back, Liam felt less like a person and more like a season. Entertaining, dramatic and ultimately lacking resolution. The kind of connection that looked promising in the trailer but never made it past the pilot.

The recurring theme? These men were easy on the eyes and about as emotionally stable as a houseplant in a wind tunnel. Every time I thought I'd met someone who might see me—like really see me—they'd turn out to be more interested in protein powder or whether their Instagram followers had gone up.

I was definitely drawing a 'type'; fun, charismatic, mildly allergic to feelings. Like emotional tumbleweeds rolling into my life, stirring up a little dust, then vanishing into the wind without so much as a proper goodbye. There was a part of me—maybe a small, deeply caffeinated part, that believed I could be the one to fix them. I thought if I were sparkly enough, kind enough, cool enough—maybe, just maybe, one of them would finally choose me.

They didn't. And looking back, with all due respect to their future selves and wives - Thank goodness!

They were like a fast roller coaster ride—exciting, unpredictable, but once you get off, you're left with a stomach full of regret and the lingering question: "What the heck just happened?"

Through all of this, I kept telling myself that I had to find the right person, the one who could fill the emptiness I'd been carrying. I chased love like it was a destination. As if once found, everything else would fall into place. Looking back now, I realise I was always running. Running from the truth, running from myself, running from the idea that maybe I was the one who needed to be whole before anyone else could ever truly fit into my life.

I always believed, despite the pain and confusion in these relationships, that this time would be different. This time, I could make it work. This time, I could change the narrative. But repeatedly, I found myself in the same pattern, the same heartbreak, the same endless cycle of trying to fix something that wasn't mine to fix.

And when it all came crashing down—as it always did—I blamed myself. I twisted myself into knots, trying to be enough. If he pulled away, I chased. If he was distant, I worked harder. And when he shattered me, I picked up the pieces and told myself I'd be better next time.

Then, like a bad dream on repeat. Sometimes, the outbursts of anger and rage returned and I found myself in the same toxic cycle. Déjà vu. If it kept repeating, surely it had to be me. And in some ways, yes—it was partially me. But that never made the abuse okay. I had just normalised it. It was the kind of love I had come to expect—volatile, unpredictable and laced with highs and lows. I was lost, the storm tossing me about with no visible escape.

And yet, despite all the pain, I continued. Because not continuing meant admitting that I had spent all that time, all that energy, all that love… for nothing.

I wish I could say there was one defining moment when it all clicked. Some grand epiphany where I walked away with my head held high, fully aware that I deserved more. But it wasn't like that. Not even close. It was a slow, smouldering, realisation (and that's putting it mildly). A quiet knowing that crept in over time and took root deep within me.

This wasn't love. This was self-destruction dressed up in romantic, youthful ideals.

My script was unravelling, gradually.

Even as I was drowning, I kept convincing myself I was fine. Treading water, gasping for air, smiling through the exhaustion because I didn't want to admit that I was sinking. Maybe I had been sinking for a long time.

And the worst part? I did not know where to go from there. If love wasn't the answer, then what was? If pursuing relationships wasn't the answer, what should I do with all this emptiness and this deep desire to give which remained unseen and unreturned?

I had spent so long believing that happiness was just one right relationship away that I had never stopped to consider that maybe… maybe I was looking in the wrong place entirely. Maybe my mission to find love was just a distraction from something deeper. Something I had been avoiding for years.

Maybe I wasn't supposed to be the one writing the script at all.

Maybe there was already a story written for me, one filled with love far greater and truer than anything I had ever chased before.

But I was too lost and preoccupied by my pain to notice. Either that, or I was just one slow learner.

By now, you may be thinking, surely, she's woken up by now? But no. My journey was just beginning. And sometimes, there's a rock bottom before there is an up.

The funny thing is, if I had just stopped running for a moment—if I had let myself be still, really still—I might have heard the truth whispering beneath all the noise. That the love I was searching for wasn't in a man, nor in the fleeting rush of infatuation. That it had been there all along, just waiting for me to turn around and see it.

But I wasn't ready.

And so, I kept running. Kept writing chapters in a book that wasn't leading me anywhere. Kept searching for love—everywhere but up.

LOOKING FOR HIM IN ALL OF THEM

"For he satisfies the longing soul, and the hungry soul he fills with good things."
Psalm 107:9 (NLT)

CHAPTER 3

RED FLAGS AND ROSE-COLOURED GLASSES

Ah, the rose-coloured glasses. If you've ever been in a toxic relationship, you'll know exactly what I mean. It's that moment when your heart is so wrapped up in emotions and idealised fantasies you fail to see the flashing neon signs warning you about the trouble ahead. Maybe you find yourself there now, or looking back. Either way, I've been right there with you, shoulder to shoulder, through the tough times. It's almost like you enter this magical thinking where you truly believe that love can fix everything, that people can change, and that, deep down, they just need to be loved the right way. Let's face it: We all want to believe the best in people—even if it's at the expense of our sanity and well-being.

But here's the thing: Ignoring red flags isn't something that only happens to "other people." It happens to us, the strong ones, the smart ones, the ones who think we're immune to manipulation or control. We think we can fix the situation or smooth over the problems. And that's the beginning of the downfall.

LOOKING FOR HIM IN ALL OF THEM

Let me take you back—to a moment that quietly began to fracture my illusion.

I was standing in the kitchen, barefoot on cold tiles, holding my phone like it weighed a hundred kilos. He'd gone silent again—no explanation, no response, just radio silence after a heated conversation where I'd dared to express how I felt. I remember looking at the screen, waiting for the dots to appear. Waiting for something. And in that awful quiet, I heard a voice inside whisper what I had tried to drown out for months: This isn't love.

But the crazy part? I still tried to justify it. I told myself he needed space. That I shouldn't have pushed. Maybe if I'd just said it differently things would've landed better. I was so wrapped up in the idea of who he could be that I couldn't accept who he actually was.

That moment in the kitchen definitely wasn't the final straw in that relationship; no, I went back for more, but it was one of many similar circumstances. I should have recognised the red flags for what they were: warning signs, not minor flaws to overlook, which I'd somehow trained myself to ignore. That I had chosen to ignore. That's how strong the pull of those rose-coloured glasses can be. Even when we know, often we still stay. Because sometimes hope feels more comforting than the truth.

I want to break this down for you because I've been in the trenches. I know how easy it is to fall into this trap. The rose-coloured glasses are often so blinding that we can't see the red flags waving right in front of us. Let's take a look at some of those warning signs we choose to ignore, and why we do it. Don't worry, I realise this is a heavy topic, but I promise not to go full doom and gloom on you. As challenging as these things were to walk through, it's kind of wild (and a little beautiful) to sit here now and realise I can talk about them with a touch of humour. That wasn't always the case. Back then, it was about as dark as it gets—in my heart, in my head. But time and grace have a funny way of flipping the script.

These are just some of the red flags I've encountered—and trust me, there are more. Not every person you meet will display all of these signs, but when it's toxic, the pattern is unmistakable. These warning signs are usually subtle at first, like small cracks in a perfect facade, but over time they grow into something harder to ignore. You might catch yourself thinking, "Maybe it's not that bad." And sometimes, it's not. But more often than not, these cracks are telling you something important about the inside-out nature of unhealthy relationships.

I've seen these red flags—and more—more times than I care to admit. They tended to follow me like an unwanted subplot through different relationships. And it wasn't until I sat down to write this to you that I realised just how much I've learned from it all. As painful as those experiences were, looking back, I can say that they were worth all the upheaval and pain, if it helps someone else avoid the same heartbreak. If sharing this helps someone feel seen or understood, or even saves them from toxic scenarios or worse, then I can honestly say it was all worth it. Because we don't always learn the lesson in the moment, but in hindsight, the clarity is undeniable.

As I reflect on all of this, I'm reminded of how easy it is to get caught up in those fantasies. It's like we forget to look at the facts. We get so wrapped up in who we want someone to be that we ignore who they really are. I convinced myself things would improve or that I could handle it, only to realise later I was falling into a trap.

That said, let's talk about more of these red flags. But let's be clear—I'm not here to hand out blame like party favours. This chapter isn't about pointing fingers at the other person. It's about turning the mirror gently inward and asking, why were we drawn to the story in the first place? Because, the real twist in the plot? Sometimes the red flags felt like home. It's not about painting them as the villain and us as the victims. Because the actual work isn't just in recognising unhealthy patterns in someone else—it's in recognising what in us responded to them. What part of our story made that dynamic feel familiar, or even safe? The attraction was never just about them. It was about the wounds we hadn't yet healed. Are we ignoring the signs? Are we choosing to hold on to something that's not good for us because it feels easier or less painful in the short term?

So, without getting too heavy, let's dive into some of the most common signs. These are the kinds of things that, if you're paying closer attention in your relationship, might have you thinking, 'Hmm… something here just doesn't quite add up.'

The Sneaky Red Flags We Overlook
The Constant "Misunderstanding"

Do you ever notice how they always seem to "misunderstand" you? It's like you're speaking two different languages. You express a concern, and suddenly, they turn it into your problem, your "overreaction," or, better yet, your miscommunication." Wait, what? I just said I don't like the way you speak to me. I didn't say you're a horrible person!"

But somehow, it gets twisted. Suddenly you're the one apologising. This is a classic display of emotional manipulation.

Why do we ignore this? We might convince ourselves, "Oh, maybe

I wasn't clear enough," or "I probably am overthinking things." It's easier to blame ourselves than confront the possibility that the other person isn't listening or truly respecting our feelings. Trust me, I've been there. For a long time, I apologised for things I didn't even do. All because I didn't want to face the reality of the disrespect. Looking back, it's almost laughable—if it weren't so painful.

But here's the kicker: These little miscommunications don't occur in isolation. They're a pattern. Over time, you'll notice that every single conversation seems to end in you defending your feelings, explaining yourself, or justifying your actions. It starts to feel like you're walking on eggshells—constantly second-guessing everything you say or do. That is emotional control at its finest. It's the kind of thing that wears you down so much, you begin to doubt your own perspective. And the longer you stay, the harder it becomes to see clearly.

I'll be honest with you: This type of manipulation is so subtle that when you're in it, you think, "Hey, maybe I am just too sensitive." The truth is, no one should make you feel like you are crazy for simply expressing yourself.

The Charm That Fades Fast

Oh, you'll likely know this one. They woo you at the beginning—charming, attentive, affectionate. It's like they're reading from a manual on how to make you feel like the centre of their universe. Then, as time goes on, the mask slips. The over-the-top compliments turn into passive-aggressive remarks. The long conversations become short answers and silence.

Why do we ignore this? Because we're addicted to the charm. It feels good to be admired, to feel like we're important. And let's be real: we don't want to believe that the person we've invested such time in is suddenly turning into someone else. We don't want to admit that we fell for their trick of thinking they were perfect when they were just using "love bombing" to hook us in. The love we feel can be so intoxicating that we put up with things we'd normally not tolerate.

In my case, I ignored the signs because I didn't want to feel foolish for falling for someone who wasn't truly interested in treating me with the respect I deserved. I didn't realise that perfect beginnings often hide shaky foundations.

Here's the thing: Charm is often a mask for insecurity or manipulation. When someone is trying too hard to convince you they're perfect, it may be because they know they have a lot to hide. We all want to believe that they're genuinely that great. In reality, that kind of all-consuming adoration is often a strategy to keep you hooked long enough to get what they want. And the worst part is, by the time you realise it, it's like trying to take off a bandaid that's been stuck on for months.

The Emotional Roller Coaster

One moment they're all in, showering you with affection, and the next, they're distant and cold. Their mood swings are unpredictable and you're left wondering, "Is it me? Did I say something wrong?"

This is the classic push-pull dynamic. One minute you're their favourite person, and the next, you're practically invisible. It becomes such a confusing, draining cycle that leaves you second-guessing yourself.

Why do we ignore this? We get used to it. You rationalise: "Oh, they're just stressed from work," or "They've been through a lot lately." You convince yourself that it's temporary and that you can help them over it or through it.

But, in truth, this emotional inconsistency often signals deeper issues—whether it's manipulation or an inability to regulate emotions. The highs feel good; we hold on, hoping to avoid the lows. But emotional instability in relationships can wear you down until you no longer know who you are outside of the drama.

And here's something I didn't want to admit at the time: I liked the highs. When they were affectionate, loving and present it made everything else feel worth it. It was the emotional equivalent of being starved and then finally getting a bite to eat. But the thing is, that's not love. Love should not be a roller coaster. No relationship should feel like being strung along or left dangling over a cliff one day and pulled back up the next.

Red Flags of Physical Abuse

I know this part is heavier, but it's essential to address because physical abuse is one of those areas where we might second-guess ourselves or overlook signs. Especially when we don't have a history of abusive relationships. We may not recognise the early red flags for what they are. Sometimes, we dismiss the warning signs as "just a bad moment" or convince ourselves that it's not that serious because it didn't leave a mark. But harm doesn't need to be visible to be real. Often, it starts subtly—control masked as concern, anger disguised as passion. And by the time it escalates, we're already entangled in justifications and confusion. That's why we have to talk about it—clearly, honestly, without shame. Recognising the signs early can make all the difference.

The Threats That Aren't Really Joking

Let's get real: jokes about violence or threats might seem harmless, right? It might start off as playful: "If you do that again, I'm going to strangle you." When does it stop being funny and start being concerning? When it's consistent. When there's no real remorse.

Why do we ignore this and brush it off? "Oh, they didn't mean it. They were just kidding." But the truth is any person who feels comfortable making threats—no matter how "joking" they seem—is often testing boundaries, seeing how far they can really push.

I'll never forget the time I heard a comment like that and laughed it off because, at the time, it didn't seem serious. But deep down, I knew it wasn't right. If something feels wrong, even if it's in the form of a joke, it's worth paying much closer attention to.

The dangerous thing is that these jokes often come before more serious behaviour. A person who jokes about violence will often escalate to more controlling behaviour when they see you brush it off. It might start with a joke, and the next thing you know, it becomes a pattern—guilt-tripping, intimidation, then even physical restraint.

The Physical Restraints

This can start small. They grab your arm when you're trying to walk away. They physically block you from leaving. It's subtle at first. You might brush it off and think, "Maybe I was overreacting." Or tell yourself, "It's nothing, just a one-off." But in reality, this kind of behaviour is often the beginning of a deeper pattern of control that can escalate… and fast.

Why do we ignore it? We downplay it. We second-guess ourselves.

We tell ourselves it's not that serious, or that it won't happen again. But in reality, these early red flags are often warnings of what's coming.

And it doesn't stop there. These small signs are often just the beginning. Once they realise that you've allowed them to physically control your space—however subtly—they'll start pushing further. What you once brushed off as a "small incident" eventually can become something much more dangerous.

Now, I must pause and really emphasise something here. I know some descriptions I've shared above might come across a little matter-of-fact—maybe even clinical. But let me be clear: what's operating beneath the surface is far more layered. There's often something much deeper, darker and more sinister at play.

Anyone moving through the world from a place of emotional, physical, or spiritual abuse—whether giving or receiving it—usually carries wounds far heavier than those visible on the surface. The behaviours may seem obvious, even outrageous. The roots? They're tangled and complex, buried in places often untouched and unresolved. Deep roots that need to be gently, but firmly, pulled out—and that's true for all of us. But especially for someone who exhibits this kind of harmful behaviour toward a friend or partner.

Let me say this clearly: This is not something you can heal through your love. It's not something you can fix with your compassion or wait out with your patience. No amount of tolerance, empathy, or sacrifice will change someone who isn't willing to change themselves. And it is not your job to try.

Your job is to take care of you—your heart, your body, your mind, and your spirit. Your job is to set the standard for what you will and won't allow in your life. Abuse, in any form—emotional, physical, or spiritual—is never justifiable. It is never excusable. And it is never okay.

You deserve more. Period.

The Narcissist—A Sneak Peek

Alright, let's dip into the weird world of narcissists for a moment, but this will be a casual stroll into narc territory—just a light preview, no emotional hazmat suit required. Chapter 5 contains the complete unravelling (brace yourself, it's a ride), but let's start with a little preview for now.

Here's the thing: this part of my story was personally life-changing. I'd had my fair share of toxic relationships—maybe even ones that leaned narcissistic—but this one? This was the wake-up call. Before I even knew what a "narcissist" was, I was already deep in it. And oh, was I in for a nightmare? Sometimes, I believe God slightly increases the volume when you don't initially catch the lesson—because a louder wake-up call is the only way to finally shake you out of it. When I say it shook me—I mean, it shook me right up. My world turned inside out, flipped twice, and left me wondering which way was up.

So, narcissism. It's one of those things that, when you first bump into it, it hits you like a bucket of cold water. You didn't even see it coming. Suddenly, there you are. Wondering how you ended up in this strange, manipulative mess. Now, there are two flavours of narcissism: covert and overt. And let me tell you, both will leave you spinning. But here's the kicker—whether it's covert or overt, it's still abuse. And no one deserves to be stuck in that cycle. But…

some of the narcissistic behaviour? Well, it's the next level. I mean, there's a whole other level of unbelievable for this stuff.

Let's start with the covert narcissist. The type who wraps their manipulation in the softest of packages. They present to be the most empathetic and caring person in the world. Someone who truly understands you. They will claim to understand what you're going through. They'll be there with a shoulder to cry on, offering advice (that conveniently always centres around their own experiences). At first, you think, "Wow, you're so thoughtful. You really know me. You get me in a way no one else does."

And for a while you think everything's fine. You think they're just being such a good person. But eventually, you start noticing cracks. You start feeling drained. You begin to question yourself: "Am I too sensitive?" They're the ones who always need something—your time, your energy, your support—but when it's your turn to ask for something, suddenly they're "too busy" or "too overwhelmed."

Here's the sad reality: their needs are always the priority. You become so accustomed to putting their needs first that you forget your own. Before you know it, you're so exhausted. You can't even remember what your needs feel like. And that's the trap. It's like being stuck in a fog. You start second-guessing yourself, wondering if you're just imagining things. But, hey, you're not.

And trust me, narcissism can be both subtle and overt. So, if you're dealing with a covert narcissist, you're in for a subtle but draining experience. They'll try to make you feel guilty for having emotions that don't align with theirs. They'll use your vulnerability against you, twisting it until you start believing you're the problem, not them. And by the time you realise what's happening, you'll be so tangled up in their web that untangling yourself feels impossible.

But hang on, narcissism isn't always so sneaky. Enter the overt narcissist—the more obvious, in-your-face kind. You know the type. They walk into a room and make it all about themselves. They don't hide their need for admiration or control; they flaunt it. Making sure you know just how great they are and just how much better they are than everyone else. But you will soon learn you're just a pawn in their game, where they see themselves as the rulers.

Now, while covert narcissism can be sneaky and take a little longer to spot, overt narcissists are usually more obvious. But don't get too comfortable just because you've recognised them—they can still be incredibly manipulative in their own right. They'll turn everything into a competition. They'll belittle you to make themselves feel superior. The best part? They'll do it so confidently that you'll start to doubt your own worth. That's how they control you, through sheer arrogance.

And here's the kicker for both types: when things get tough, whether it's an argument, a disagreement, or a moment of vulnerability, they always make it about themselves. Your pain? It's just an opportunity for them to say, "Well, I have it worse, you know." The minute things get difficult, they flip the script. You could go through a breakup, losing a job, or facing a health crisis—and somehow, suddenly, it's their pain that's the priority.

I've seen both types up close more times than I'd like to admit. And let me tell you—it's exhausting. It's like being trapped in a cycle where nothing you do seems good enough. You start questioning your reality. Wondering if you're just too sensitive. Or if maybe, just maybe, they're right. That's the power they seemingly have over you—the power to distort your reality until you're unsure of what's really happening.

But here's the deal: whether covert or overt any form of narcissism is incredibly toxic. And the reason it's so life-changing to recognise this behaviour is because it opens your eyes to how much we ignore, justify, and rationalise in our relationships. We ignore those early signs, thinking that love can fix it. Or that things will get better if we just try harder. But when you're dealing with narcissism—whether subtle or obvious—it never gets better on its own. It only gets worse.

I won't go too deep into this just yet—I'm saving the juicy details for Chapter 5. But for now, take a moment to reflect on what you've read here. Are there any warning signs you've been ignoring? Are you giving too much of yourself and wondering why you feel drained? Or maybe you're constantly questioning your worth because of someone else's need to control or belittle you?

I've been there. I know just how painful and confusing it can be. But once you see these patterns you'll never unsee them. And let me tell you—recognising it is the first step in freeing yourself from the manipulation. When you finally take off those rose-coloured glasses, you'll be able to see things for what they truly are. And that, my friend is a game-changer.

Removing the Rose-Coloured Glasses

Now that we've surveyed some of the biggest red flags—those flashing lights you've probably been ignoring—I want to leave you with something: You don't have to ignore them anymore!

When we look at relationships through rose-coloured glasses, we do ourselves a disservice. We ignore the red flags that are trying to protect us. Ignoring them doesn't make the problems go away—it just delays the inevitable. You're not crazy for seeing them; You're not imagining things. You just have to get brave enough to take off the glasses and see the entire scene clearly.

I get it. It's not easy. Trust me when I say: You deserve a healthy relationship, not one that makes you doubt your worth or reality. Looking back, I understand how much I intertwined my identity with being the one who could stay, forgive, and fix. But healing doesn't come from proving your loyalty to someone else's brokenness—it comes from showing that same loyalty to yourself.

"For God is not the author of confusion, but of peace..."
1 Corinthians 14:33 (KJV)

"My grace is all you need. My power works best in weakness."
2 Corinthians 12:9 (NLT)

PART 2

THE BREAKING POINT

---

*"This hope is a strong and trustworthy anchor for our souls.
It leads us through the curtain into God's inner sanctuary."*
Hebrews 6:19 (NLT)

CHAPTER 4

THE FIXER TRAP: WHEN HELPING BECOMES HIDING

For a season my heart felt brave—noble, yet burdened and unbearably heavy. I became the silent saviour in stories no one asked me to write. I wore a quiet badge of honour no one asked me to carry—the role of the Fixer. Looking back now, I see it for what it was. A deeply rooted, trauma-driven pattern of trying to heal others as a way to avoid my own healing. I didn't know then that I was living inside a trap—one that offered temporary purpose but ultimately robbed me of my peace, my power, and my potential.

On the surface, being a fixer looks like compassion. It looks like patience, loyalty, even love. You see someone broken, someone hurting, someone lost. So you throw yourself into the rescue mission with everything you have. Believing in their potential, you hold on to the vision of who they could become and make their healing your project. And if you're anything like I was, you tell yourself; "This is what love is. This is what faithfulness looks like". But underneath it all is something far less beautiful—a hidden ache, a history of abandonment, a belief that if I can make him whole, then maybe, finally, I will feel whole too.

The fixer trap didn't start in adulthood. For me, it started early in life. I internalised the idea that love could be earned through being useful. If I were the good girl, the strong one, the one who made life easier for others, then maybe they wouldn't leave me. That belief followed me like a shadow into every relationship I entered.

There was yet another recurring character I stayed tangled up with for far too long. You know the type—one of those characters that somehow keeps getting written back into the story, even though the plot really doesn't need him anymore.

Our connection was fast, loud, and dramatic—like a car crash you can't look away from. I mistook chemistry for calling. I mistook intensity for intimacy. I thought the spark meant something. (It didn't!)

He was charming, magnetic, and wounded (to say the least). I saw pieces of myself in his pain which somehow made me feel connected. He carried emotional wounds from his past—rejection, cycles of failure, abuse and a sense of lost purpose. And in true "fixer" form, I grabbed my metaphorical toolkit and got to work. I listened to every story. Affirmed every insecurity. Supported and encouraged him, but slowly morphed into an unpaid therapist with romantic feelings. Meanwhile, my sense of self quietly exited stage left.

I didn't want to leave him behind, so I gave up opportunities. I downplayed red flags like I couldn't see them—even when they were waving right in front of me. I bent my boundaries into strange little shapes trying to keep the peace. And every time I thought about ending it, a voice whispered, "If I go, who will love him like I do?"

The truth? I needed someone to believe in me.

I was pouring everything I had into someone who wasn't even asking for healing. And I ignored the screaming signs. I was slowly fading. I convinced myself this was growth. That he just needed more time. That I was being strong, patient, and loyal. But in reality, I was just exhausted and running on empty.

The reality? I rarely left. These relationships didn't end with clean breaks or satisfying closure. They just kind of… faded. Like a terrible movie with a confusing plot and no resolution. Just a scene cut short. Yet somehow always available for a sequel I didn't seek.

And because I never properly shut the door—it left just enough of a gap for him to reappear months or years later—script in hand, ready to recast me in the leading role of a storyline I should've closed the curtain on long ago.

And still… It felt like a death. Not just of the relationship, but of the version of me who believed that was all I was worthy of, despite the time, energy and effort committed.

The fixer. The helper. The one who stays.

Comfort in Chaos

Here's the twisted part of the fixer trap: It feels safe. When you're so used to living in survival mode dysfunction can feel like home. There's a strange comfort in focusing on someone else's pain. It deflects the mirror away from your own. It gives you a reason to delay your own healing.

I found solace in the story I was telling myself: I was doing a good thing. I was being strong. That person needed me. Those justifications, however, masked a deep-seated insecurity. I was afraid that if I stopped trying to fix him, I would have to face the parts of me I didn't know how to fix.

And so I clung to the chaos. Not because it was worthwhile or good for me, but because it was familiar. Because I equated love with pain. Effort with worthiness. Suffering with purpose.

Avoidance Masquerading as Loyalty

The most dangerous part of the fixer trap is that it wears a mask of loyalty. You tell yourself you're being faithful. That real love stays. That you're honouring God by sticking it out. And yes, love is patient. Yes, grace is real. But love does not require you to lose yourself.

I had to face the painful truth that my "loyalty" was actually avoidance. It was easier to focus on his brokenness than confront the emotional patterns keeping me bound. Easier to support his dreams than pursue my own. Easier to hope for his healing than to address my own.

And it wasn't just one relationship. It was a pattern. Contrasting faces, same dysfunction. Each time I believed, "This time will be different." But I wasn't different. I was still operating from the same wounded place.

Roots of the Trap

Digging deeper I realised my fixer trap stemmed from early beliefs I'd adopted—moments where I felt valued for being helpful. Times when strength was celebrated while vulnerability was ignored. I learned to silence my needs and show up for others, even when it cost me everything.

That belief followed me like a script: If I can help them heal they will stay. If I can be their saviour, they will love me.

But no one created me to be anyone's saviour. That's not my job—and it never was. Only Jesus can do that.

The Illusion of Control

Another layer of the fixer trap is control. When you feel powerless in your own life trying to fix someone else can create the illusion of authority. You feel needed. You feel in charge. You think you're steering the ship—but the storm isn't theirs, it's yours. And you're the one going under.

Trying to control someone else's journey will never heal your own wounds. And trying to earn love through performance will only leave you emptier than you are already.

In hindsight, I can see how the hand of God was guiding me—even when I didn't recognise it. He was there all along. I was just too blind, too naïve, too wrapped up in my striving to notice.

Still, He stayed—ever-present in the background, gently redirecting my path while honouring my free will to keep making the same mistakes on repeat.

Because that's what genuine love does. It doesn't control. It doesn't force. It doesn't manipulate.

It waits.

It stands by faithfully—your greatest cheerleader—whispering through every closed door, every red flag, every sleepless night: "Wake up. Turn around. There's more for you than this." But never overstepping. Never violating your personal choices.

Ever so gently, He attempted to show me my self-worth wasn't contingent on my ability to fix others. That I was worthy of healing, not just handing it out. That there was something beautiful, bright and wildly redemptive up ahead… if only I'd noticed the stop sign and chosen to turn right instead of left.

The ultimate GPS—gracious, patient, and unwavering—just waiting in the background, ready to lovingly reroute me toward a future filled with more hope, healing and purpose than I ever thought possible.

From Fixing to Freedom

These days I still love deeply. I still see the gold in people. But I no longer carry the burden of being the saviour. I've learned to set boundaries. To let people own their own process. To honour my healing journey above someone else's needs, personal demands and timeline.

There is such peace in surrendering the fixer role. In trusting God with people instead of trying to be their god. In realising that genuine connection doesn't come from fixing, but from being.

Being whole.

LOOKING FOR HIM IN ALL OF THEM

Being seen. Being loved for who you are—not for how much you can rescue.

The fixer trap is seductive, especially for women who've been told that love is a sacrifice at all costs. But genuine love starts with wholeness. And healing begins when you turn inward, not outward.

So, if you see yourself in these words—if you've been the fixer, the rescuer, the one who always shows up for others at the expense of yourself—know this: You are allowed to heal. You are allowed to rest. You are allowed to stop fixing.

There's a version of you on the other side. Whole, free, flourishing and loved. She doesn't need to save anyone to be worthy of love. She already is.

> *"Above all else, guard your heart, for*
> *everything you do flows from it."*
> *Proverbs 4:23 (NIV)*

CHAPTER 5

ROCK BOTTOM AND REEBOKS®

The Descent Disguised as Destiny

There are chapters in your life that feel like war zones. But this one? This felt like ground zero to me. It was as though everything had been blown to smithereens before I even realised I was within the blast radius. I call it "rock bottom," but to be honest, that feels far too poetic, too gentle. This was rock bottom times 100. This wasn't just a bump in the road; it was like someone threw me off a cliff blindfolded. Convinced me I could fly, then blamed me for the crash landing.

It started like one of those quirky indie rom-coms. The kind where two unlikely characters cross paths and fate takes it from there. Except instead of a whimsical montage and a heartwarming ending, it turned into a psychological thriller with a twist I never saw coming. He came in like a lovable rogue—a real-life version of the charismatic guy from every Aussie pub. Not my usual type, not even close. But that made it exciting, right? He had that larger-than-life energy. A lovable larrikin. Life of the party that sucked you in before you even knew what was happening. Charismatic.

LOOKING FOR HIM IN ALL OF THEM

Loud. Full of banter. You know, the kind of guy everyone says is "a good time," but your spirit is quietly whispering run, babe, run.

I thought this was it. The final chapter of the fairytale. My overdue happy ending.

Except of course, it wasn't.

It was the beginning of the wildest descent into the emotional, spiritual, and mental chaos I had ever known.

Looking back (and I write this over a decade later) the signs weren't just there—they were practically skywriting. Blazing red flags, gut punches dressed as intuition and divine warnings that hit like holy megaphones. Words like 'emotionally bankrupt' didn't just whisper—they roared through my spirit like sirens, begging me to wake up. But love—or what I thought was love—has a funny way of making you blind. Or worse, willingly oblivious. Being the committed little soldier of romance, I remained determined this plane could fly. Successfully convincing myself I could turn a nose-diving aircraft into a private jet headed for forever. Too starry-eyed to see that this was no divine appointment—it was a spiritual ambush.

It started with a "friendship," they always do. That familiar slide from platonic to problematic. He wasn't my type, but he was magnetic. And my wounds? Oh, they were right on schedule. Drawn in, like moths to a flame. It didn't take long before the love-bombing began—multiple pairs of Reeboks, grand declarations, an intensity that screamed forever but was actually just a fast pass to a very dark place.

At first it felt like the real deal. Fast, fun, passionate. I remember thinking, finally. This is what it's meant to feel like. He made me feel chosen. Special. Like this wasn't just another chapter—this was the whole damn book. But the pace... oh, the pace! It was like being on a bullet train with no brakes. And the faster we went the harder it became to slow down to see clearly. Things sped up from there, I mean fast. From "friends" to "something more, meet the parents" speed. And part of me—maybe the wounded part—thrived on the intensity. I thought intensity meant connection. That chaos meant passion. That being constantly dizzy with confusion meant I was just "falling hard." Oh, honey; I was falling alright—straight into a vortex of manipulation, lies and psychological warfare.

Looking back, I was feeling something powerful. Something I believed was love. At least by that definition I understood back then. But I wasn't in love with him. I was in love with the idea of who he could be. Who he pretended to be. What I hoped the story could become. I was in love with the potential. The way he made me feel in those fleeting, love-bombed moments when it felt like I was the only woman in the world. Multiple pairs of Reeboks later, I was practically hypnotised. Trauma bonding? Hadn't heard of it. Narcissist? Couldn't have spelled it.

The first cracks were subtle. Little inconsistencies. Unexplained absences. Vague responses. Then came the "friends" who felt a little too familiar. Other women whose names kept circling back like unwanted boomerangs. Stories that didn't quite add up. And yet, I kept choosing to believe the fairytale. I had invested big time. Emotionally, spiritually, mentally. I wanted it to be real so badly, I ignored all the glaring signs it wasn't.

Then came the day everything unravelled.

It was a random Tuesday night—I remember it so clearly because I was sitting in my room with my laptop open, trying to distract myself while he was overseas. He was meant to be away on a "boys' trip" in Canada, the US, but social media told a different story. There he was. Tagged. Smiling. With another woman. Not just any woman. THE woman. The one I had been told was "just a friend."

My heart didn't just break. It imploded.

I felt like a freight train had hit me. Numb. Confused. Shocked.

But it wasn't even just about the photo. It was about the avalanche that followed. Like a dam had broken, and all the hidden truths came rushing at once: mutual connections, whispers turned into confirmations, messages, screenshots, receipts.

Turns out, I wasn't the only character in this play. Not even close. I was one of many. A placeholder. A pit-stop.

The realisation hit hard, and with it came the spiral.

I remember sitting there, jaw clenched, chest tight, scrolling through article after article about narcissistic abuse. I didn't even know then what 'narcissist' meant. Not really. But as I read, every line felt like someone had shadowed our relationship and turned it into a psychological case study.

Love bombing. Check. Gaslighting. Check. Triangulation. Check. The charm, the chaos, the control. Check, check, check.

I had been a frog in slowly boiling water, but now it was scalding.

What followed were some of the darkest days of my life. I stopped eating. I stopped sleeping. I was an anxious mess: My mind a maze I couldn't escape. I felt like I had lost myself. My reality. My sanity. Every single relational wound I had ever experienced resurfaced, bleeding, screaming for attention. I wasn't just heartbroken—I felt fractured.

And yet, somehow, beneath all the debris, there was this faint, almost invisible glimmer of something I hadn't felt in a while.

Hope.

Not loud. Not obvious. But there.

I call it "My Little Hope." A seed planted long ago. Buried so deep it took hitting rock bottom to even realise it was still alive. It didn't roar. It whispered. *You will survive this.* But at that moment? Of course I didn't know how.

That part comes later.

Right now, this is the part of the story where everything breaks. Where the fairy tale ends not with a kiss, but with betrayal. Where devotion becomes devastation. Sitting in the rubble, you wonder how the heck you got here and if you'll ever feel whole again. It may feel like the story ends here, but buckle up—there's more madness before the breakthrough. Because this was just the beginning of this storm.

The Discard—Take One

As I sat there unravelling the craziness of the situation, inside me was screaming out—this subhuman excuse for a human being is a fraudster, a fake. I had just been a victim of a hijacking. Emotionally, spiritually, physically, psychologically. But hang on—so had the woman in Canada. She was flying blind, just like I had been. But now, she was in my old position. She was the flavour of the month (quite literally). She did not know what she was dealing with. No clue I even existed. If she only knew what he was doing. What he had done. How he left me on the other side of that flight completely convinced we were "fine" and that he'd be back in a few weeks from the "boys' trip".

Then came the Facebook deletion.

I still remember the sharp sinking feeling when I saw he had removed me as a friend in mid-air—mid-air! Who even has the emotional capacity to do that at 30,000 feet? Then came more photos. Pictures of him and her—the "new woman" he'd apparently lined up like a backup singer, just waiting to take the mic. The level of audacity next - level. Something out of a soap opera, but not even your standard weekday drama. This was *Days of Our Lives* on steroids with a dash of *American Horror Story!*

And me? I was the unwilling extra, getting dragged through every hellish scene.

It wasn't just heartbreak. It was the kind of pain that rewires your brain. The type of betrayal that doesn't just sting—it disorients. I wasn't just dealing with a breakup. I was dealing with an identity crisis. Who was I to believe someone like this? How did I not see it coming? How could he just go on as if nothing happened while I was here in a mental, emotional, and spiritual heap on the floor?

In those days, I could barely hold a thought without spiralling. I'd walk into a room and forget why I was there: Look at strangers and wonder if they could see it. See the betrayal, the abandonment, the fresh scar tissue holding me together.

Nights were the worst. Nights made me a philosopher and a forensic investigator all at once. I'd lie in bed, replaying every conversation. Trying to pinpoint the exact moment he turned. Did he ever really love me? Was I just a placeholder? A training ground? A layover en route to his next emotional victim?

That's when the obsession started.

I deep-dived into the world of narcissism like my life depended on it—because, in some twisted way, it felt like it did. I devoured articles, watched YouTube videos. Followed therapists on Instagram like they were celebrities. I learned about love bombing, trauma bonding, and gaslighting. And oh, did it all click. This wasn't love. It was a performance. And I had been cast without my consent.

What no one tells you is that even after you understand what's happened—even when you know they're toxic, dangerous, damaged—there's still that ache. That longing. The "but why" that clings like smoke to your skin.

Because I wasn't pretending. I was in it. I loved deeply. I had dreams. Future plans. Joint goals. I had bought into the illusion. My emotions were real. That's the part that makes you feel like a fool.

So, I tried to rebuild.

I reconnected with friends whom I had unintentionally pushed away while I was caught in his whirlwind. I read every self-help book that had a vaguely empowering title. I worked out like it was going out of fashion. Every step was like a reminder: You are still here. You are still breathing. You haven't been destroyed.

But it was hollow.

Because while I was doing all the things I was "supposed" to be doing to heal, he was gallivanting around America like the villain in some travel-themed rom-com. There were beach selfies, dinners, overly romantic captions. And her—the new woman—beaming like she'd won some emotional lottery.

And I wanted to scream: RUN. I wanted to tell her; *Lady you don't know what's coming!* You don't know that he will use you. Drain you, then discard you too when your shine wears off. And part of me hated that I cared. But another part of me—the one with the stubborn hope still clinging to my ribs—wanted her to see the truth before she ended up like me.

Weeks turned into months. I was patching myself together with affirmations, prayer, and (let's be honest) carbs. I was determined not to let this break me permanently. Tears were now scheduled on alternate days. A sign, surely, that I was on the up and up.

He was dead to me. Photos? Deleted. Blocked? Everywhere… except on the phone—I know, don't even ask!

And then… the message came.

Back in the Lion's Den

The infamous hoover. It was like watching a horror movie and hearing a knock on the door you know no one should open. And yet some sick curiosity pulls you to the doorknob. I had read about this. I had prepped for it. The textbooks, the videos, the digital cheerleaders in the narcissist recovery groups had warned me recently: They always come back.

Even so when it happened it knocked the wind out of me.

He didn't apologise. Not properly. Of course not. Narcissists don't do genuine apologies. He threw out vague lines like "I never stopped caring" and "I was going through so much." Classic deflection. Classic bait. Just enough to reel you back in, but never enough to take real accountability.

And yet—a sick part of me wanted more. Answers. Closure. Some glimpse of remorse. Justice. More than that, I needed the truth. I wanted to hear him say what he had done. Acknowledge it. Own it. But deep down, I knew I was waiting for a level of self-awareness that did not exist in that shell of a person.

Outwardly I was all strength and sass. I rolled my eyes. Scoffed. Told friends I'd never speak to him again. Internally? Well, there I was in a war zone.

Because the thing about these kinds of betrayals is that they leave you questioning yourself much more than the other person. And when they reappear, it shakes all the ground you just spent weeks or months trying to stabilise.

I went into lockdown. Not the government-issued kind. The emotional kind. I stopped trusting my gut. I double-questioned every decision. My confidence took a nosedive. Was I still that naïve? That desperate for clarity? That willing to revisit the crime scene?

Apparently, yes.

Because the mind craves answers, even when the spirit knows better.

That was the darkness. Not just the betrayal, but the battle within myself. The fight between knowing the truth and craving the lie. Between what I deserved and what I still thought I wanted.

And the scariest part? The realisation that I was still vulnerable to him.

I wish I could tell you I walked away for good. That I finally blocked his number. Healed my trauma. Booked a Bali retreat and met a kind-hearted barista named Jake, who loved dogs and never once gaslit me.

LOOKING FOR HIM IN ALL OF THEM

But no.

Instead, I walked right back into the lion's den but this time; The lion didn't pounce. He lured me in. Whispered sweet nothings laced with deceit.

Caution or wisdom did not mark round two as one would hope. Exhaustion marked reality's blurred lines and such desperation to believe in the fantasy I thought I'd finally woken up from. Turns out, I'd just hit snooze.

You might be reading this with a hand over your face, wondering how someone could fall for it all over again. Trust me, I was wondering the same thing—in between panic attacks, gut instincts I silenced, and late-night "this time feels different" journaling.

He returned from overseas with a new act. Same script, different costume. I asked questions. I poked holes. I even convinced myself I was just being cautious when really, already I was halfway down the rabbit hole, clutching a flashlight and mistaking it for discernment.

This wasn't reconciliation. It was psychological warfare disguised as a reunion. The curtain rose, and I stepped back into the role I thought I'd retired—leading lady. Reprising my role in a script I once believed would end in joy, only to be met with plot twists and emotional whiplash.

And here's the thing. He almost had me convinced he was self-aware. That the mask had come off and we were going to do it right this time. There was even that one conversation where he alluded—ever so subtly—that he might have narcissistic traits or Narcissistic Personality Disorder. You'd think that would be the red flag to end all red flags. But for me it felt like progress. Like, wow!

He knows! He admitted it! Maybe that was the turning point I'd been waiting for.

It wasn't of course!

Because in hindsight, that 'confession' wasn't humility, it was strategy. A calculated move. Just another manipulation designed to lure me back into the role he'd always cast me. The redeemer. The rescuer. The one who could 'fix' what he never intended to heal or reform.

And was I ever committed to the role.

The Second Discard and the Darkness

Believe it or not, I actually started planning our future again, right in step with his newfound 'commitment'. He promised the whole white-picket-fence package. Even talk of buying the dream house in my favourite suburb, just to seal the illusion. Family holidays. Even babies. (Yes, babies. I wish I were kidding) Everything that he'd resisted before was now part of the pitch. No hesitation. No distance. He was all in—supposedly.

But here's the thing: when a narcissist offers you the world, it's usually because they're about to drop you off the edge. It's not love. It's preparation. Something like emotional fattening for the slaughter. The love bomb before the final blow. And you never see it coming— not because you're stupid, but because you're still hopeful.

And hope, in this kind of relationship, is the most dangerous drug of all.

I wasn't naïve. I had some walls up. I'd done my late-night research. Watched the YouTube therapists. Read the blogs. Even dabbled in the odd trauma recovery podcast while walking my dog around the block. Pretending my life wasn't a waking soap opera. I knew what narcissism was on paper—but knowing it academically is not the same as living it.

I was still asking the questions. Still searching his eyes for anything real. Still measuring every answer like I was examining a crime scene. Piecing together the forensic remnants of a man I once believed in.

And even though I knew, deep down, that this was a house of cards built on gaslighting and manipulation—I was still there. Still waking up beside the lie and calling it love.

Because here's what no one tells you: when you are trauma - bonded, the abuse starts to feel familiar. Safe, even. Like a broken - in pair of shoes that give you blisters, but you keep wearing them anyway. Because it's what you know. Because at least it's something.

There were days I looked in the mirror. I didn't even recognise myself. My sparkle had dulled. My humour—once quick, witty, and electric— subdued. I wasn't myself. Far from it. I was a version of myself that had been emotionally mugged, spun through a psychological washing machine, tumble-dried with shame.

But hey, I smiled in the photos. We even started talking about wedding rings and "next steps." He was playing the role. Reformed villain. I was back to believing this whole twisted love story would finally get its "Hollywood ending".

Dream on babe!

Because then came… The Second Discard.

And I tell you, if the first one broke me, the second one nearly buried me - quite literally. This wasn't just your average breakup. This was a calculated annihilation. A punishment. The discard to end all discards.

Remember, narcissists don't just leave you. They dismantle you.

And how did this final blow land? Simple. He withdrew everything—emotionally, physically, mentally. All that warmth? Gone. Poof. Just like that. He disappeared—gone, gone. Gone! Missing in action. No explanation. No words. Just silence. Complete and utter silence. And, to add that final sick twist, it happened right on cue on my birthday weekend. Of all weekends, right? The weekend away he had booked as if to add insult to injury. Probably for the drama. Just to twist the knife deeper. The ultimate discard. The crème de la crème of all discards. Ghosted on steroids. No warning. No fight. Just gone!

And here's the thing—this time, I wasn't just confused. I felt obliterated. Shattered doesn't even begin to cover it. The experience reduced my mind, body, and spirit to rubble. My nervous system? Destroyed. I could barely breathe. I couldn't even process what had just happened to me. The silence that came with this discard? It was like a weight pressing down, suffocating me. Cold. So cold it made the first discard feel like a mere inconvenience. The kind of cold that freezes your very core. This time, he wasn't just gone for a few days. He was gone. Really gone. Off to the next victim (swiftly validated) undoubtedly with an entirely new version of the truth. Painting me as the villain in his story. Meanwhile I stood lost amidst the wreckage. My mind raced to understand what had just happened. I won't weigh you down with every scene from this emotional dramacide—just know it was the kind of chaos that leaves a deeply traumatic imprint.

LOOKING FOR HIM IN ALL OF THEM

The mask? Completely gone by now. The actual monster was finally revealed. Speaking with fluent cruelty. As if I had wronged him. As if I were the villain in his warped little tale.

And me? There I stood in the wreckage. Gazing at shadows of what remained of me. Rock bottom had taken on entirely new meaning. I never thought I could hit a place so low. There I was—completely broken. This wasn't just the end of a relationship. This was the end of the fantasy. The nightmare ending to my long-winded quest for the fairytale. Turns out my Prince Charming was a subhuman master of illusion, to put it nicely. So, where did that leave me? What did that make me? The answer wasn't as clear as I had hoped. But one thing was certain: Finally I'd reached the wake-up call I'd needed all along. That one I couldn't ignore anymore.

And maybe that's what stung most. Not the loss of him—but the loss of my dignity. The realisation that I had put myself back in harm's way. That I had chosen the same fire and expected not to get burned.

It felt like an emotional suicide.

My mind was a battlefield. Some days I'd replay everything and wonder if I was crazy. Other days I'd mourn the fake future he promised, like it was an actual death. I yelled at the ceiling. I googled therapists. I wrote long, unsent texts, trying to make sense of it all. I deleted them. Rewrote them. Like a madwoman I danced between rage and heartbreak. My body felt the strain too, frozen, as if it couldn't keep up with the chaos. Most days, getting out of bed felt like my body had aged a lifetime, as if the trauma had seeped deep into my bones. And through it all, there was a spiritual toll, as if my mind, body, and spirit had been shattered—because, in many ways, they had been.

And I was angry—not just at him, at myself.

How could I fall for it again?

But then, slowly, as the fog started to lift the most painful truth settled.

I hadn't been loved.

I had been used. Played. Exploited. Recycled.

And that's a hard pill to swallow when you give someone the deepest parts of you—your body, your laughter, your dreams, your trust. And they treat it like garbage. Like a game. Like a disposable tissue they could wipe their mess on and toss in the bin.

It's not dramatic. It's true. Narcissistic abuse isn't love gone wrong—it's love that was never real on their end to begin with. It's spiritual, emotional, physical, sexual and psychological abuse.

And when you wake up? When it really clicks?

You don't just grieve the relationship. You grieve for yourself. The girl who believed. The woman who tried. The heart that hoped.

And in that place of grief… is where the real healing starts.

The light part? The flicker of hope in the rubble:

Even amid that mess. Even at that lowest point. I began to hear a new voice. Not his. Not mine. Something deeper, more divine. A whisper that said, This isn't the end. This simply is the unmasking.

This wasn't about heartbreak. It was about excavation. Digging up all the broken beliefs I had about love, worth, and loyalty. About what I tolerated and why. About who I was before he came in like some ominous destructive whirlwind.

LOOKING FOR HIM IN ALL OF THEM

And slowly, piece by piece, I began to rebuild. Not for revenge. Not to prove anything. But because the darkness had shown me something precious. My resilience. My ability to rise, even when everything told me I shouldn't be able to. And that? That was my actual miracle.

"I'll never forget the trouble, the utter lostness...
it's a good thing to hope for help from God."
Lamentations 3:19-23 (MSG)

"When you pass through the waters, I will be with you...
when you walk through the fire, you will not be burned."
Isaiah 43:2 (NIV)

CHAPTER 6

THE BREAKING BEFORE THE BREAKTHROUGH

The Lighthouse

There comes a point in every journey where the noise of the world quiets just enough for the soul to hear itself. That moment, though often quiet, can feel like a collision—the soft breaking of a heart that's finally too tired to keep pretending.

No man could heal what was broken inside. Not even the good ones. That was the turning point—the moment the illusion shattered.

You see, when pain becomes your compass, you start following broken paths as if they're the only roads that exist. I had become so accustomed to surviving that I'd forgotten what it meant to simply be.

And in that survival, I had clung to relationships that mirrored my pain back to me. Unhealthy. Unkind. Manipulative. Toxic. They were familiar. They fit my wounds. They gave my dysfunction a place to breathe.

LOOKING FOR HIM IN ALL OF THEM

But then...

In the middle of that emotional wilderness—right when the noise was loudest—something unexpected happened.

Or rather, someone. A divine interruption to my destructive life rhythm.

He wasn't new to me. He had been part of my life before—many years prior. The first time we crossed paths, something about him lingered with me long after. It wasn't some fireworks-laden moment. No romantic whirlwind. It was subtle. Gentle. But profoundly different from anything I had experienced.

This person was different. So different, in fact, that even the memory of him still carries a certain light. He wasn't perfect, no one is, but there was a purity in our connection. It was simple, gentle, and unforced. It was the kind of presence that made my heart smile, rather than race with anxiety. He was tall, dark, handsome, sure, but more than that he had heart. Kindness. Humour. A stillness that disarmed life's obvious noise.

There was a depth to him. A kindness that wasn't performative. A sense of safety that didn't require explanation. When we spoke I felt heard. With him, I felt seen. Not for the mask I wore but for the person beneath it. He never tried to fix me. He didn't pressure me. He just... "was". Present. Authentic. Warm.

Looking back, it was the first time I felt what a healthy male energy could be. No games. No manipulation. No motives. Just a simple connection that made my heart smile.

But I wasn't ready.

He appeared like a glimpse of what "healthy" could look like. But

I was in no place to receive that kind of love. I didn't know what to do with someone who didn't need me to "fix them". The irony of his presence—then and later—was almost cruel. Because as much as I admired him, cared for him, respected him… I couldn't receive what he represented.

I wasn't in the right place.

Peace, gentleness, anything resembling safety did not calibrate with my broken parts. My nervous system didn't know what to do with calm. Chaos was my addiction. Familiarity had taught me that love looked like volatility and pain. That relationships are earned, not rested in.

So, I pushed him away. Not in any overt or dramatic way. But quietly. Subtly. I just didn't step toward him. I let the space widen. I didn't trust myself to hold something so pure, so rare.

After our first encounter, life moved on. I moved on. At least, I pretended to. I buried the memory, the regret, the possibility. Then, years later—during that very dark season of my life—he reappeared.

I was in deep at that time. I mean deep, at the deep end. Entangled in that toxic relationship that left me drained, confused and lost. That kind of situation where the soul knows it needs to run. Yet the body stays frozen. Entangled in the mess of manipulation and emotional chaos. I had become someone I barely recognised. I knew the relationship was bad but I was stuck. It mirrored the brokenness I had never dealt with.

And in the middle of that, there he was again. Like a lighthouse on a cliff, beaming into the storm.

I don't even think his return was romantic. It didn't need to be.

LOOKING FOR HIM IN ALL OF THEM

He showed up like a signpost from God. A flag in the ground. A moment that whispered: *You still have a choice. This isn't all there is.*

He reminded me, not by words but by presence, that there was still goodness. That not all men want to take. That love doesn't always come dressed in chaos. And yet—even with his presence, I couldn't leave the toxic relationship: I was in far too deep. My heart wanted freedom, but my trauma still chose bondage. I could feel myself slipping further even as my spirit longed for air.

I don't know what prompted it. Maybe it was divine timing. Maybe it was God throwing a lifeline when I was seconds away from going under. Either way, it felt surreal. Like a dream. Here he was again. Just as kind. Just as grounded. Just as quietly present.

But I was far too deep in the abyss.

I was entrapped. Someone who embodied every unhealthy pattern had me emotionally shackled. I felt exhausted, numb, ashamed. And even though this person—this light, this reminder—stood right there, warning me of the storm ahead… I couldn't stop the nosedive.

I ignored the lighthouse.

This wasn't the first time God had sent me a sign. But this one hit differently. There was a special part in my heart for this man—not because I idolised him, but because his presence reminded me of something sacred. Something I forgot existed. Something I didn't think I deserved. Even just a few brief encounters with him stood out among a lifetime of toxicity and noise.

I believe God sent him—twice. Not to save me, but to remind me. To reveal a gentle contrast. A glimpse of what health and wholeness could look like. But also to show me clearly that no man could heal me. Not even the good ones. That work had to come from within. That surrender had to be mine.

And even though I didn't listen at the time, the seed was sown.

Eventually, the breakdown came. The inevitable crash after years of trying to outrun myself. And it was in the ruins that finally I found the truth.

It was an inside job.

And I resisted. Oh, how I resisted. I remember that pull inside me. That emotional resistance to truth. Because truth means change and change is terrifying when brokenness is all you've ever known. I felt afraid. Scared to fail. I feared that letting go of familiar pain would leave me with nothing.

A Saviour I Couldn't See

Deep down, I knew. I knew that even this man. This kind and loving presence couldn't save me. If the best version of love still couldn't reach the dark corners of my soul then what could?

That was the moment. The breaking before the breakthrough. The realisation that healing couldn't come from the outside. It had to begin within.

I couldn't run anymore. I finally saw the truth: I had made love an idol. I had made people my saviours. My attempts to earn worthiness had exhausted me.

But there, amid the wreckage, came a whisper.

There was no grand epiphany. No lightning bolt from the sky. It was subtle, quiet. I just remember hitting a point where the pain of staying the same became greater than the fear of change.

I remember admitting, maybe for the first time, that I couldn't do it anymore. That I didn't have the strength. That I didn't want to keep repeating the same cycles. That something had to give.

That was the day I began to turn.

It didn't all change overnight. But the shift started with that single, trembling step. My acknowledgment came from an understanding that only I could choose differently. With surrendering the illusion that someone else will save me. Not the narcissist. Not the man with a kind heart. Only One had the power to restore me from the inside out.

God had been waiting all along. And even though I took the long road—bruised, battered, scarred—He welcomed me home. Not with judgement. But with open arms. With redemption.

Not to a place. But to a person. The One who has been with me all along, weaving Himself through the tapestry of my mess. The One who had given me the freedom to choose, to wander, even to destroy, but never once withdrew His redemptive plan.

That's the thing about God. He doesn't control. He doesn't force. He loves, waits and He redeems.

He knew my plan before the beginning of time. He knew the mistakes I'd make. The detours I'd take and He planted people along the way—like this one incredible person—to serve as signposts. Gentle reminders. Warnings. Invitations.

And that man—maybe he will never know how much his presence meant. I don't even think he was aware of how much light he carried into my darkness. He was just being himself. Kind. Honest. Steady. But to me, he was more than a memory. He was a miracle.

You see, when your soul is cracked open, even a whisper can feel like a roar. And God whispered through him.

It wasn't immediate, my turnaround. I still had more falling to do. But the seed was now sown. The awakening had begun. And as I slowly began to walk away from the toxic situations—as I started to look inward instead of outward. I came face to face with the One who had been waiting all along.

The One who could actually heal me.

Not a man. Not a relationship. But Jesus.

I had always known Him, in theory. Grew up hearing His name. But in that season I met Him in a new way. Not as a religion. But as redemption.

He didn't shame me. He didn't scold me. He just held me. Slowly, He showed me my worth. Piece by piece, He put me back together again. I learned to forgive myself. To grieve the lost years. To let go of the need to be chosen and start choosing myself—through Him.

And that amazing man? He faded into the background again, his role was obviously complete. He was a divine appointment, a lighthouse. And I'll always be grateful. For the way he made me feel safe. For the way he reminded me that goodness exists. For being a gentle echo of God's love in a season when I could hear only confusion and clamour.

To this day, I carry that moment. When I realised the answer was never in them, but in Him - Jesus. When I stopped running toward people and started running back to the One who created me. When

LOOKING FOR HIM IN ALL OF THEM

I stopped looking for a saviour in human form and returned to the Saviour of my soul. And it changed everything.

If You're There Now...

If you're reading this and you're where I was—if you're stuck in a place that feels dark, addictive, chaotic—if your heart has been so fractured you're not sure it can ever be whole again…

Let me tell you something real. No one is beyond redemption. You are not too far gone. There is always a way out. And you don't have to have it all figured out to take the first step.

But that step? It starts within. It starts with letting go of the illusion that someone else will save you. It starts with surrender.

Healing is hard. But so is staying broken.

Choose your hard road.

Because one will keep you imprisoned. The other, eventually, will set you free.

And just like He did for me, God will meet you in the middle. He'll send reminders. Gentle lighthouses. Unlikely messengers. A lyric in a song. A stranger's kindness. A dream that brings healing. A sudden stillness in the chaos. Something will stir in your spirit—like hope trying to rise again.

You don't have to be ready. You don't have to be strong. You just have to be willing. Willing to be seen. Willing to be loved. Willing to try again.

The breakthrough begins with the breaking.

The rebuilding begins with surrender.

And please hear me—You are worth the rebuild. Every scar. Every story. Every silent prayer. He has seen.

God hasn't forgotten you. You're not invisible to Him. Even in the pit. Even in the relapse. Even in the numbness. He's been reaching for you all along.

And now? This might just be your moment. Not the finish line, but the beginning. The first flicker of light after a long, dark night.

Take the step. Breathe again. Let the healing begin.

> *"Even when their paths wind through the dark valley of tears, they dig deep to find a pleasant pool where others find only pain. He gives to them a brook of blessing filled with the rain of an outpouring. They grow stronger and stronger with every step forward."*
> *Psalm 84: 6-7 (TPT)*

> *"And I will give you a new heart, and I will put a new spirit in you.*
> *Ezekiel 36:26 (NLT)*

PART 3

THE BREAKTHROUGH

"Who is this one? Look at her now!
She arises out of her desert, clinging to her beloved.
When I awakened you under the apple tree,
as you were feasting upon me,
I awakened your innermost being with the travail of birth
as you longed for more of me."
— *Song of Songs 8:5 TPT*

CHAPTER 7

THE LOVE I NEVER KNEW

There are moments in life that divide everything into a "before" and an "after". For me discovering the true love of Christ was one of them. It didn't happen overnight. It wasn't in stained-glass perfection or some ethereal out-of-reach experience. It happened slowly through my brokenness. Through the unravelling. Through the pain I tried so hard to run from. Through the searching I didn't even know I was doing.

For most of my life, I thought I understood love. I thought it was conditional. Something you earned. I thought it depended on performance, appearance, remaining small enough not to cause waves. I thought love was tolerance at best and abandonment at worst. I learned to equate love with inconsistency, with apologies, with betrayal. And perhaps without even realising it - I projected all of that onto God.

I thought Jesus was distant—a figure up in the clouds, holy, unreachable. I believed He was real, yet I didn't believe He would be personal. Not with me. Not in the mess I had created. And while I held on to the idea of faith, it felt like something reserved for the polished, for the well-behaved churchgoers who knew when to raise their hands and when to sit back down. Faith felt like rules and God felt like a far-off principal who noticed only when you messed up.

But oh, how wrong I was.

You see, there's a love you can't fully grasp until you meet the One who is love itself. Not just loving. Love. The very definition of it. The very source. The very breath.

When I began to truly open my heart to Jesus—when I surrendered not just the pain, but the pride, the illusion of control, the broken belief systems that were driving my life—everything changed. Not in a dramatic flash of lightning or a booming voice from heaven. But in the stillness. In the moments where my soul was finally quiet enough to hear Him whisper: "I'm here. I've always been here."

And that whisper? It changes everything.

I realised then that what I had been longing for all along wasn't a man, or a high, or an achievement. I was aching for something tangible, yes, but not from this world. I craved a presence. A steady, constant, ever-knowing presence. What I didn't know was that I was craving the Spirit of God. A spirit that is real. Tangible. Not some far-off concept or mythical idea. He is not boring. He is not cruel. He is not cold or distant. Certainly not judgemental. He is the most alive, captivating, comforting presence you will ever know. He is beyond your wildest dreams.

And the best part? He is wildly in love with you.

This isn't about religion. It's about relationship. It's about connection to the very One who formed your soul. God is not a thing.

LOOKING FOR HIM IN ALL OF THEM

He is a person. And He's not a distant one, either. He is present. Real. Close. His spirit is closer than your breath. And when you encounter His presence—really encounter it—you are never the same.

There is no addiction strong enough. No trauma is deep enough. No wound is painful enough to keep you from that love. And not just any love. A holy, burning, transformational love. A love that heals. A love that fills every void you thought would never close. A love that restores your identity, one truth at a time.

I spent so many years seeking after men who couldn't carry the weight of my soul. Who were empty themselves, yet I expected them to fulfil me. I didn't realise it then, but I was connecting my spirit to something that wasn't whole. It could never satisfy me because it was not designed to. We were never made to find completion in another person. God created us to be connected to Him first. His spirit is the blueprint. The root. The home.

Somehow, we got it backwards. We go to everything else first, and God last. We try to patch our brokenness with temporary fixes and earthly answers. Too blind to see that the real longing is Divine and eternal.

I know what it's like to feel like God is far away. I know what it's like to think you have to be perfect, or put together, or fixed before you come to Him. But that's not who He is. God doesn't love the filtered version of you. He loves the real you. The raw you. The 'you' that can't hide behind your highlight reel.

He is not like the people who left. He is not like the ones who abused, rejected, or manipulated you. His love is not harsh. It is not critical. It is not conditional. It is pure. Gentle. Kind. And completely unwavering.

When I understood the true nature of God's heart, it undid me in the best possible way. The walls I had built to protect myself crumbled. The fortress I had used to survive became unnecessary. Because I had finally found the One who saw every corner of my soul and still chose me.

And the truth is, He's choosing you too.

Maybe you've been waiting for something to change. For someone to come rescue you. For the pain to stop. For the answers to come. But, friend, the breakthrough begins with the breaking. It starts when we stop running and start receiving. When we surrender the illusions and grab hold of the truth. That we are already loved. Already chosen. Already pursued by a love that has no strings attached.

He's not behind a cloud in a faraway place. He is here. Right now. And though He will never force His way into your life, He is always knocking. Always waiting, always hoping finally you will open the door and let Him in.

There's a verse in Revelation that says, "Behold, I stand at the door and knock. If anyone hears my voice and opens the door, I will come in." He doesn't say, "If you're perfect" or "If you've got it all together." He says if you hear and open. That's it. It's an invitation. One that leads to healing, wholeness and purpose.

There is a love I never knew until I finally stopped trying to be strong. Until I finally let Him in. And in that letting in, I found the most real, most raw, most radiant connection I had ever known. A connection that wasn't based on my performance, but on His promise.

It was in those quiet, surrendered moments I discovered this truth:

God's love doesn't just patch you up. It remakes you. It restores you. It gives you a name, a home, a mission. And you don't have to strive for it. You just have to receive it.

The Hard Work of Transformation

But let's be real. Healing wasn't a switch I flicked on. Transformation took work. Deep, confronting, soul-rattling work. And it didn't start right away.

After my soul-shattering relationship left me a mere shell of who I was, I didn't magically find peace, Jesus, or happiness. No. That relationship nearly destroyed me. I was far from recovered, even after escaping the chaos.

I didn't have some great spiritual awakening the moment I left. I was in survival mode. The kind where you breathe, but barely. The kind where you pick up what pieces you can and try to keep moving because standing still would mean feeling too much. So, I did what many of us do: I threw myself into something else.

My first business became that 'something else.'

Launching that business felt like reclaiming something I had lost. My voice. My independence. My future. I felt like I was at last pursuing a dream I'd had but couldn't pursue while with him, because I was too weighed down. I wasn't healed—not even close—but I was determined to never go back. I refused to let anyone else dictate my worth anymore.

It's possible I used the business as a diversion, but at least it wasn't another toxic person. And that was a win. In fact, my business became the new number one in my life—and I was more than okay with that.

There still were a few hiccups with men during that season. One in particular stands out—someone who could've become another painful chapter. But I had changed. I had boundaries now. I didn't let him in. Not fully. Not deeply enough to wound me again. And even though I was still working through trauma, I had a fierce resolve not to repeat the devastating past.

That season taught me something powerful: minor victories count. Saying no when you used to say yes. Walking away when your heart still wants to fix it. Choosing silence over chaos. Choosing you—finally.

I always felt destined for something more. That there was a bigger purpose, a Divine thread in my story. And as I poured myself into building my dream, something else built quietly behind the scenes—hope. That "Little hope", buried long ago.

Then, around 2019, something shifted. It was like the Lord began knocking a little louder. I can only describe it like this: I had been running wild and free like a brumby in the open fields, and now I could feel His whisper in the wind. "It's time."

Not in a restrictive or condemning way. But like a gentle invitation. A loving nudge. He had let me run for a while—reclaiming, rebuilding, rediscovering—but now, He was calling me deeper. Into healing. Into wholeness. Into the next layer of truth.

And then came COVID. The stillness. The global pause. Everything slowed. And in that silence. He spoke.

He began to meet me in a new way. Not just as Rescuer, but as Restorer. Not just as Father, but as a friend. Not just as Saviour, but as Lover of my soul. And little by little, the pieces came together—not perfectly but Divinely.

And that's the thing about transformation. It doesn't always come in loud, cinematic ways. Sometimes it comes in the quiet. In the daily choices. In the decision to get up and keep going. To keep healing. To keep growing.

Every little step mattered. Every "no" to the wrong thing. Every "yes" to the right one. Every time I chose rest over hustle. Surrender over striving. Truth over fear. It all added up. It all changed me.

The Awakening

It wasn't dramatic. There was no booming voice from the sky or blinding light. It was quieter than that. It was subtle, gentle—like the morning sun slowly lighting up a darkened room.

Around the time the world shut down during COVID, something in me shifted. The chaos outside only made the stillness inside more noticeable. With nowhere to go and everything stripped back, I sat in the silence—and that's where it began.

God started to change the desires of my heart.

At first I didn't even notice. I was still living life on the surface. Still tangled in striving and trying to figure things out on my own. But my appetite for the things I used to crave faded. The things that once entertained me, soothed me, distracted me no longer held the same weight. I felt this slow, steady pull—a drawing. Not toward religion or rules, but toward a person. I didn't know how to explain it. It felt like He was changing me from the inside out.

And I wasn't resisting.

For the first time, I didn't feel like I had to fix everything. I didn't have to have all the answers. There was a strange peace, even though

I was still wrestling with a lot. The striving lifted. The anxiety I carried like a second skin didn't feel so heavy. I was still unfolding, still asking questions—but now I wasn't doing it alone.

Slowly, gently, He answered.

He started revealing the truth, not all at once. Not in any way that overwhelmed me, but piece by piece. Like puzzle pieces being laid down in front of me. I would hear something or read something, and suddenly it would click. I'd remember a moment, or a Scripture, or even some subliminal message I once may have brushed off and it would take on new meaning. I realized He had been speaking all along. I had just never learned how to listen.

There was one moment I'll never forget. I was sitting alone, the world still quiet in the strange stillness of lockdown. I wasn't even praying, just being. And in that stillness, I felt a wave of something I hadn't felt in a long time—peace. Not the kind the world gives. Not the kind that comes from finally figuring everything out. But the kind that settles deep in your spirit and whispers, "You don't have to carry this anymore."

That was the beginning of trust.

God was undoing things in me I didn't even know needed unravelling. Bit by bit, He showed me where I'd built my life on half-truths. Where I'd been performing for love. Where I'd attached my identity to things that were never meant to define me. He did it kindly. He didn't rush me. He just kept showing up, gently guiding me into the truth.

I became hungry for more of Him. Not just knowledge—though I had a lot of questions—but a relationship. Intimacy. I wanted to know His heart, not just His hand. I wanted to be with Him, not just use Him to fix my own personal circumstances.

LOOKING FOR HIM IN ALL OF THEM

Looking back, I see now that He was awakening something in me—not just saving me from something, but calling me into something. He was beginning a transformation that would take time. But even then, the shift was undeniable: Slow, yes, but real.

He was giving me fresh eyes to see, a new heart to feel and a new appetite for truth, for righteousness, for Him.

And though I didn't have all the answers, I had something better.

I had Him.

The Hope

If you're still in the middle of your process—still learning to breathe again, still finding your voice—please know: you are not behind. You're being rebuilt.

God's love isn't just about rescue. It's resurrection. Revival. Rebirth. It is the very power that takes every ounce of your pain and turns it into purpose—the purpose hell cannot stop.

And He's not finished with you.

If your heart is heavy. If your spirit feels cracked. If you're sitting in the middle of your own unravelling, may I remind you? You are not alone.

There is a love waiting for you that surpasses anything this world can ever offer. It isn't manipulative. It doesn't ghost you. It doesn't fail you. And it doesn't shame you. It simply saves you.

This love is a person. His name is Jesus.

He is the love you didn't know you needed. The answer to the ache you couldn't name. The home your soul has been longing for.

If religion, people, or pain have given you a distorted view of God—I hope this chapter gently invites you to reconsider: Maybe He's far more beautiful than you've been told. Perhaps you've just scratched the surface. Maybe your real journey with Him is only just beginning.

> *Because when you begin to know the heart of God, you start to grasp the love of God. And when you understand His love, you encounter His presence. And when you encounter His presence; you are never the same.*
> *- Simone Cassell*

You were made for this. You were created for His love. You were designed for His Spirit.

Let Him in.

He's waiting. And He's everything you never knew you needed.

> "Do not fear, for I have redeemed you; I have summoned you by name; you are mine."
> Isaiah 43:1 (NIV)

> "For my thoughts about mercy are not like your thoughts, and my ways are different from yours. As high as the heavens are above the earth, so are my ways and my thoughts higher than yours."
> Isaiah 55:8-9 (TPT)

CHAPTER 8

HEALING THE GIRL IN THE MIRROR

Author's Note:
This chapter contains references to the life and story of Gabby Petito, whose tragic loss deeply moved me. I share this reflection not to speculate, but to honour her memory and shed light on silent forms of abuse. My intention in sharing this reflection is not to sensationalise her story, but to honour her legacy and speak to the silent pain many endure. If sharing my experience can help even one person recognise their worth and walk toward healing, then this story will have served its purpose.

Gabby

I didn't expect a true crime documentary to unravel me on a balmy summer Saturday. It was supposed to be background noise—kettle on, dishes stacked and a documentary playing in the background. One of those (sadly) true stories Netflix serves up when you're not emotionally prepared to be cracked open.

It was the footage of Gabby Petito, the police body cam video from that traffic stop before she disappeared. At first, I just watched with concern. But then, something hit me like a freight train.

I looked up from the sink and locked eyes with Gabby on the screen, and everything around me just…stopped. The infamous police body cam footage was playing—the one where she's pulled over, nervously explaining herself, brushing tears off her cheeks while trying to downplay what had clearly just happened with her fiancé. I heard her voice. Soft. Shaky. Apologetic.

The more I saw of her, the way her voice trembled while she apologised for things that weren't her fault. The way she twisted herself into a version of calm that only trauma survivors know how to perform. Then she cried with this heartbreaking mix of fear and hope—I suddenly felt like I was watching a ghost of my younger self.

And it hit me.

Not just emotionally—viscerally.

Her pain, posture, panicked smile… It was like staring straight into a mirror: Me at around the same age. In her trembling voice, I didn't just hear her—I heard echoes of my own. Of the young woman I had been. Of the girl I once was. Learning to normalise the abnormal. The girl who didn't know yet that fear wrapped in romance is still fear. I knew that look. That strange blend of confusion and shame. The internal calculation of "How much of the truth is safe to tell right now?"

Right there in my kitchen, clutching a tea towel, with tears welling. I wanted to reach through the screen, hug her, look her in the eyes, and say: "Sweet girl, please run. This isn't love. And you do not have to stay. Please don't apologise for his brokenness. Please live!"

LOOKING FOR HIM IN ALL OF THEM

It chilled me to my core. Because I knew. I knew what was really going on in that footage. And I knew that look in her eyes because it used to be mine. Fear, wearing the mask of "I'm okay." Sadness disguised as self-blame. The way she tried to protect him. The way she took the blame. The way she bent herself in so many directions just to make the moment feel less terrifying.

I'd done that. Been there. Lived that.

I watched the officers—kind, perhaps, but clueless—and I wanted to scream. Can't you see? It's right there! Written across her body in a language, screaming in plain sight. I was furious. Grieved. And haunted by the reality that she didn't make it out.

What happened to Gabby wasn't just terribly tragic—it was familiar. Because the enemy that tried to destroy her had once set its sights on me. While our stories ended differently, the emotional battlefield she stood on felt all too familiar. That moment didn't just trigger old wounds—it revealed how far I'd come. It was a turning point. For a long time I had buried parts of my own story labelling them as shame or survival. But seeing Gabby. Seeing the version of me I had long tried to forget. It was as though God gently pulled those memories back up. Not to torment me but to remind me that I hadn't just made it out, I'd been entrusted with something.

Her story pulled my healing into the light and made it matter in a whole new way. A new revelation. It reminded me that my survival wasn't just a stroke of luck—it was a stewardship. A calling to use what I've lived through, hopefully to help speak life into someone else.

Gabby was an undeniable light. A beautiful soul. That same enemy I'd fought tooth and nail in my own life was the one who hunted her. And that made me mad.

But that moment also ignited something in me. A holy fire. A righteous rage. A deep, soul-stirring responsibility. Something happened in that moment, and I realised then: If my story, my scars, or my voice can reach even one girl like her, then I have to speak. Not just for healing—but for honour. Her life mattered. Her light mattered. And no one had the right to extinguish it.

If I could share just one part of my story that might reach a girl like her, someone who feels too ashamed, too afraid, too entangled to escape—how could I not? Not out of ego. Not because I've "arrived." But because I know what it's like drowning in a sea of manipulation and calling it love. And I know just how rare lifelines can be, unless someone's brave and determined enough to throw one.

Too many young girls are being swallowed whole by their "relationships". Demons that promise a life of safety and joy but deliver silence, gaslighting, soul decay, or worse. And they need someone to say, "I see you. I was you. You're not crazy. You're not too much. And you absolutely deserve to live." If only I could reach through time and whisper to Gabby what I know now—that the pain wouldn't last forever. That there was still beauty waiting ahead. Sadly, I couldn't reach her or rewrite her story—but maybe I can help someone else start a new chapter.

At that moment, watching Gabby's story unfold became a strange breakthrough for me. It was as if God whispered, "Now do you see? This is why I brought you through." I realised that healing isn't just a private restoration. Watching Gabby stirred something deep inside me. Her story helped me recognise I wasn't just healing from something—I was healing for something. The kind of moment where purpose quietly walks into the room and sits beside you.

LOOKING FOR HIM IN ALL OF THEM

The kind where the ache transforms into an assignment. The kind where healing becomes not just personal—but generational.

I realised even more that healing wasn't just about survival. Although that may come first. It was about surrender and then embracing the purpose that comes with the pain, using it to guide the way forward. Deep down, I'd always known there was meaning in what I went through, but suddenly, after all this time, I knew it wasn't time to stay quiet anymore. It was time to speak, because there are still other Gabbys—other Simones—out there. And if sharing my story helps even just one of them that's more than enough for me.

And most of all, I wanted to tell them (my younger self included) that when your own healing takes place and when you do it with God, it becomes an incredible adventure. One full of mystery, grace, grit and surprise plot twists. (Side note: God really is the ultimate plot twist guy.) What you think would be scary turns out to be the biggest adventure of all.

Best of all, God didn't rush me. He didn't shame me. He just kept walking with me faithfully while I healed at what felt like glacial speed. And in that process—through the moments that felt ridiculous and raw—He showed me something sacred:

That healing isn't a one time milestone. It's a slow, steady becoming. It's God peeling back layers you didn't even know you had. It's Him whispering, "There's more," just when you thought you were done. It's laughing at yourself one moment and feeling completely undone the next. It's holy chaos wrapped in divine kindness.

So, no—healing didn't go the way I imagined.

It went better.

Because it went His way.

And as I reflect back on some of the struggles I've shared with you through what seems to be my long, winding journey—am I a slow learner? More than likely, but I can honestly say when you start to see the plan and purpose of God in it all, it is truly miraculous.

It's not what I thought my life would look like at almost any point. But I'm genuinely grateful for where He's brought me. In some ways in a short time compared to the years of dysfunction. But I must be clear: A healing journey is never over on this side of heaven. I don't believe it ends. I think we keep learning and when we stop… something's off.

Gabby's story was a painful mirror but it also became a compass. It pointed me back to God's faithfulness. To the progress I hadn't even realised I'd made. It reminded me that healing is never just for us—it's also for the ones still stuck in the storm. Her story, as tragic as it was, became an important turning point in mine.

Beauty in the Breaking

Looking in the mirror was one of the hardest things I've ever done. I'm not talking about the literal mirror—although, let's be honest, there were days when even that was tough—I mean the soul mirror. The one that shows you who you are beneath all the masks and titles and filters and filters-on-filters. Facing *that* version of myself? Ouch.

It was painful. It was confusing. And sometimes it felt like I was falling apart when I was actually falling into place. It took courage I didn't think I had. Vulnerability I used to avoid at all costs and surrender of control over what I thought my life should look like.

But in that surrender, God did something wild—He started changing my desires. The things I used to chase didn't appeal anymore. The people I thought would be there for life quietly faded into the background. All part of His plan. I wasn't looking for someone to complete me—I wanted God to refine me.

And as I gave Him more room in my life, I slowly realised something powerful. My past mistakes don't define me. What defines me today is how I chose to heal.

Redefining the Word "Home"

I used to think "home" was a person. A partner. A relationship: Someone to cuddle with on rainy nights and split pancakes with on Sunday mornings. And while those things can be beautiful blessings, they're not foundational.

For the longest time I tried to find peace in people. Wholeness in relationships. Purpose in being chosen. But God showed me that home isn't found in someone else's arms. It's found in His presence.

When you let Him into the places you've guarded most. He doesn't walk in with judgement. He walks in with healing.

The healing didn't come with lightning bolts or dramatic speeches. It came through daily surrender. Through tiny acts of bravery. Through choosing peace over chaos. Through learning how to sit with myself with no need to be validated by someone else.

That was my breakthrough moment. Realising I didn't need to keep striving. The Creator of the universe deeply knew and wildly loved me. And wow, once you get that revelation—whew, what a game changer!

Fuelled by Purpose

Healing didn't turn me into a perfect version of myself. Far from it! It turned me into a more authentic one. I stopped apologising for taking up space. I started creating again. Seeking my dreams. Laughing again. I began walking into rooms not wondering if I was enough, but knowing I am, because He says I am.

And here's something else I've learned: Joy is holy. Humour is healing. And sometimes God uses your messiest moments as material for your most powerful life testimony.

I used to think God wanted me to be fixed before He could use me. But no, He just wanted me to be willing. Willing to show up, cracked and curious. Willing to trust Him more than I trusted my trauma. Willing to believe that there was more ahead than what I had left behind.

And wow—He exceeded my expectations. He showed up with spiritual bonuses I didn't know even existed (more next chapter). But He didn't just meet me there—He went beyond what I knew to ask for. First came peace, quiet, but undeniable. Then clarity. The kind that clears the fog and steadies your steps. Then purpose slowly rose, sure and insistent like it had always been there waiting.

True North

Pain had rewired my GPS. By people, by poor decisions, by painful detours. But Jesus recalibrated it—not just to get me back on track, but to remind me where True North really is.

It wasn't about becoming someone's other half. It was about becoming whole in Him.

He showed me that wholeness doesn't mean perfection. It means integration. It means living aligned with your values. Walking in truth. Being honest about where you're at but hopeful about where you're going. It means being okay with not having all the answers because you trust the One who does.

And the girl in the mirror? She started smiling back. Not because life became perfect, but because she finally knew to Whom she belonged.

What I Want You to Know, Sis

If you're reading this and you're in a season of heartbreak, confusion, or just plain exhaustion, please know you're not alone. You're not crazy. You're not behind.

You're just in the middle of your story.

And if healing feels slow, that's okay. Slow healing is always still healing. Forward is forward.

But also—don't be afraid to laugh along the way. Cry, of course. Journal your heart out. But also, dance in your kitchen. Wear the lipstick. Send the funny meme. Let yourself live while you're healing.

Because healing isn't just about survival—it's about revival. It's about becoming the person you were always meant to be. Not just free from the past, but free for the future.

And when you heal in the presence of God, something even deeper happens: You dream again. You hope again. And you believe that joy isn't just possible but promised.

You stop rehearsing old wounds and start rehearsing God's

faithfulness. You stop asking, "Why me?" and start saying, "Use me!"

You rise. Again and again. And one day, you look in that mirror—not just to see your reflection—but to witness your resurrection.

Some Real Actionable Truths I've Learned:

1. Your worth isn't attached to who stays or who leaves.
2. Healing begins when honesty begins. Be real with God even if you're angry or confused.
3. Create space for joy. You're allowed to laugh while you heal.
4. Stop waiting for someone to save you. Jesus already did.
5. Choose you—with Him. Not in a self-centred way, but in a God-first, heart-guarding kind of way.
6. Pay attention to inner peace. It's a GPS signal from heaven.
7. Don't be afraid to start over. You're not starting from scratch—you're starting from experience.
8. Celebrate the quiet wins. Progress isn't always loud.
9. You don't need closure from them when you've got clarity from Him.
10. You can be healing and hopeful at the same time.

So, yes, healing the girl in the mirror took time. Still does. But I wouldn't trade a single moment, not even the painful ones.

Because in finding wholeness beyond relationships I found something far better:

I found home.

I found myself.

LOOKING FOR HIM IN ALL OF THEM

And most of all, I found Him.

And He is enough.

Always has been. Always will be!

> *"Then I will say to my soul, 'Don't be discouraged; don't be disturbed, for I fully expect my Saviour-God to break through for me. Then I'll have plenty of reasons to praise him all over again. Yes, he is my saving grace!'"*
> *Psalm 43:5 (TPT)*

> *"Forget the former things; do not dwell on the past. See, I am doing a new thing! Now it springs up; do you not perceive it? I am making a way in the wilderness and streams in the wasteland."*
> *Isaiah 43:18-19 (NIV)*

CHAPTER 9

LOOKING FOR HIM IN ALL OF THEM (AND FINALLY FINDING HIM)

There is a moment, often after years of pain, struggle and wanderings, when the chaos settles just long enough for clarity to shine through. For me, that moment came like a whisper after a storm. A quiet knowing that what I had been searching for in all the wrong places was never far from me. He had been there all along.

I grew up knowing about Him. I attended a Christian School. Found salvation at seventeen and possessed all the qualities of a girl who knew the truth. But truth without deeper understanding, or truth without revelation is just noise in the background. It's possible to know about Jesus and still not know Him. And somewhere in the gap between head knowledge and heart transformation—I got lost.

Right around the time I said yes to Jesus I also started saying yes to attention, affirmation and the lies of counterfeit love. I was looking for Him in all of them—every relationship, every flirtation, every attempt at connection. Deep down I wasn't just looking for love. I was looking for healing. For wholeness. I longed to hear that I was enough, worthy, loved. The irony, of course, is that those very things were already mine. When I couldn't access them through Christ I repeatedly sought them from people, unequipped to provide them.

Without pointing fingers at any church or denomination. I can say my experience with Jesus was undeniably real back then, but something felt missing. I lacked revelation knowledge about how to truly encounter Him on an intimate level. Looking back—I realise that absence was significant for me—perhaps for others too?

Somehow, I had picked up the idea that I had to fit a certain mould to belong in church culture. I didn't feel called to serve within traditional church walls. Deep down, I felt like I wasn't "good enough" for ministry anyway. That type of calling never felt like it matched who I was.

I had no real understanding of what it meant to discover my true calling or how God-given gifts could align with purpose. No one that I recall ever taught or preached those things. So I ended up feeling like a round peg in a square hole when it came to church and church life. There was no deep sense of belonging, not for me at least, so I went searching for it elsewhere.

The creative, wilder side of me longed for something more, something real—and at the time, I didn't believe Jesus could be part of that. I thought He was too tame, too structured, too tied up in rules and roles that didn't resonate with me. I couldn't have been more wrong!

Now I know the truth: There is absolutely nothing boring about a relationship with Jesus!

It took years—decades, even—to come to the true end of myself. To finally admit that my way wasn't working. That I was tired of being tired. That my soul was weary of striving, of pleasing, of searching.

I had no dramatic lightning bolt moment. It was more of a slow awakening. Like dawn breaking after a long night. I saw that the pain wasn't punishment. It was a pathway. That every heartbreak, every wrong turn, every toxic encounter had a redemptive thread running through it.

He was always there.

Watching. Waiting. Whispering.

"Come back."

And when I finally did, it wasn't met with shame or condemnation. It was met with love. With grace. With open arms. That's the thing about Jesus—He doesn't scold you for taking the long road, even the wrong road. He just rejoices that you finally come home.

Looking back, I can see it so clearly. Every man I chased. Every relationship I clung to… Every heartbreak I endured—all me trying to fill a void that only He could fulfil. Identity doesn't come from another person. Fulfilment doesn't come from being chosen by someone else. Peace doesn't come from getting the fairytale ending. Those come only from God.

When I finally allowed Him to show me who I really was, everything changed. Insecurity began to dissolve. Self-doubt gave way to truth. The lies I had believed for years lost power. And the most beautiful thing? I started to trust again. Not just people. But most importantly, Him. I believed that maybe—just maybe—there was a plan for my life after all. A plan far greater than anything I could have crafted on my own. That He wasn't like men from my past. He wouldn't let me down. In fact in this earthly life, He was the only one I could truly trust with my whole heart. I could bring Him the best and the worst parts of me and He would still love me—deeply, unconditionally. A kind of love that no human being could ever fully replicate. And I realised I needed that kind of love first, the love of my Creator, before I could ever receive it from anyone else.

The Joy of Purpose

Purpose isn't just about what you do—it's about who you are. And everything shifts the moment you understand whose you are. Jesus doesn't just give directions. He is the direction. With Him, nothing is wasted. Every chapter, every scar, every tear becomes part of the story that brings others to hope. I realised that the calling on my life wasn't just about healing from the pain. It was about redeeming it.

My story—messy, meandering as it is and so far from perfect—was becoming a testimony. And somewhere along the way, I found there's nothing quite like stepping into what you were created for. The joy is uncontainable. The peace—unshakable. And the love is absolutely overwhelming. It's because of His love for you that He can turn your pain into your purpose. Knowing the universe's Creator deeply loves you causes the validation you once sought from flawed people to lose its tight grip. It becomes so small in comparison to the hope, identity and purpose that were written over your life before time began. And when the pieces of your story begin to come together—when you see that even the chaos had meaning, and that He truly has a plan for your life—it's nothing short of incredible.

SIMONE ALYSHA CASSELL

Wholeness in Him

The journey from insecurity to stability hasn't been easy. No such journey ever could be! But it has been worth it. I used to question everything—my worth, my voice, my ability to discern truth from lies. But as I let Jesus rewrite those internal narratives everything began to change.

He didn't rush me. He fathered me. He nurtured me in truth until it became my default lens. And the more I trusted Him the more I could trust myself again. Sure, betrayal hurts. Disappointment bruises. But God rebuilds what was lost far stronger than before.

Wholeness isn't the absence of pain; It's the presence of Jesus. It's knowing that no matter what comes, you are anchored. That you are never alone. That even in the silence, He is speaking. Even in the darkness, He is there. I look back now and see how He was always threading redemption through my story. Even the chapters I wanted to rip out. Especially those. Because in those pages, His grace shines brightest. Wholeness isn't just about healing what's behind—it's about walking boldly into what's ahead. When you know who you are in Him you stop chasing roles and start living from revelation.

The True Love Story

This is the true love story. Not one between a man and a woman, but between a broken girl and her Saviour. A love that chased me down, then waited patiently. Never gave up on me. A love that requires no earning or proving. A love that simply "is".

God's love filled every void I thought no one could reach. It mended the fractures in my heart and breathed life back into my soul. It rebuilt what I thought was beyond repair. It gave me a new name, a new identity, a new future.

I spent so many years thinking that if I just found the right relationship, the right man, the right moment—finally I'd be okay. But every relationship I leaned on for my identity cracked under the weight of my expectations. And how could it not? I was asking human hands to hold divine burdens. Only God can love us in a way that doesn't leave gaps. Only He knows every wound and every wall—and still stays. And more than that, He heals. His love is not surface balm. It reaches deep. It rewires. It restores. It reclaims. He now calls what was once damaged "destined".

This isn't just my story of heartbreak to wholeness—it's a love story. A true one. The kind where the Hero doesn't just arrive—He rescues. The kind where love isn't earned; it's eternal. And the best part? It's not exclusive to me.

Jesus has always been the love I was looking for—in every misstep, in every detour, in every moment I thought I had to settle. He was there. Not judging, but gently guiding. Not punishing, but patiently pursuing.

If you're anything like me, you've probably spent years trying to find "the one". Let me tell you the secret: He's been there all along. And when you find Him you'll realise you were never actually lost—just waiting for Him to find you.

For You

If you find yourself where I once was—stuck, broken, confused—know this: You are never alone. And you are never beyond healing.

Unlike me, you don't have to spend decades searching for something—someone—who's been with you all along. Jesus isn't far. He's not aloof. He's not waiting for you to get it all together. He's just waiting for your "yes".

You can begin again. Right here. Right now. And it won't be boring. It won't be religious. It will be the most exciting, freeing, life-giving adventure you've ever known. A relationship, not a rulebook. A Saviour, not a system.

He sees you. He knows you. He loves you.

And He's calling you.

If you're reading this and wondering if it's too late—please hear me: It's certainly not.

If you feel like you've made too many mistakes, wandered too far—you haven't.

If you're tired of doing life on your own terms, still feeling empty—good. That's often where the greatest stories begin.

Jesus isn't a distant idea. He's not an old religious figure or a list of dos and don'ts. He's the living God. The most real thing you will ever encounter. The safest place your heart could ever land.

And He's not hiding. He's right there—waiting.

Waiting to meet you in your mess. Waiting to hold the parts of you that feel too fragile to offer anyone else, waiting to rewrite your story with grace, truth, and redemption that goes deeper than every scar.

He's not waiting with disappointment or disapproval. He's waiting with compassion. With open arms. With a love that doesn't flinch at your flaws or failures. He already knows the worst and He still chooses you. Every single time.

You don't have to clean yourself up first.

You don't need to have the right words.

You don't have to pray a perfect prayer.

You just need to be willing.

Willing to let go of what's been holding you back.

Willing to trust again.

Willing to believe that maybe—just maybe—there's more for you than what you've settled for.

Here are some truths I wish I had understood sooner:

- Your identity is not in a relationship status. Single, married, divorced or somewhere in between your worth doesn't change.
- No one can complete you but Jesus. Anyone else is a bonus, never the source.

Lessons Learned (and Lived)

Here's what I know now:

- Your identity isn't up for debate. The One who created you has already spoken over you.
- Wholeness doesn't come from another person. It starts with God and only He can complete what's broken.
- Healing is a process. But it's also a promise. And He walks with you through every single step.
- You can hear from Him. Not just through sermons or scripture,

but personally—through His words placed in your spirit, through nudges, dreams, impressions, that unmistakable inner knowing.
- Purpose isn't passive. It finds you as you move toward Him. It unfolds.
- You don't have to wait decades like I did. You can turn now. Today. This moment. And everything will begin to shift.

I know what it's like to be numb.

To smile on the outside while breaking inside.

To crave something real but not know where to find it.

To be surrounded by people and still feel unseen.

But I also know what it's like to be found.

To be healed from the inside out. To be filled with a peace that makes no sense in the natural world.

To be led by a God who doesn't just rescue you—He restores you.

So, if your heart is stirring right now, don't ignore it. That gentle pull you feel? Well that's Him.

He's not just inviting you to believe—He's inviting you to belong.

You don't have to keep pretending.

You don't have to keep striving.

You don't have to keep carrying things alone.

Let Him in.

Say 'yes'. You have nothing to lose, everything—literally everything—to gain.

LOOKING FOR HIM IN ALL OF THEM

Through life's journey I've come to realise that what we desire or think we need often is far less than the abundance God has planned for us. Our understanding and circumstances limit our vision, but God's vision is infinite. What feels fulfilling in the moment may not always satisfy in the long run. But when we step back and trust His timing and purpose, we discover that His plans are always greater, richer, and more meaningful than anything we could have imagined.

The dreams we chase can often be quite small compared to the extraordinary life He wants to lead us into, full of purpose, growth and transformation beyond what we could ever envision on our own.

One Last Thing...

If you've made it this far, through the depths of my story, thank you—truly—for being on this journey with me.

This story wasn't easy to write. Because it's mine. It's my past. My wounds. My unravelling. I've lived through nights where I begged God to take the pain away. I've walked through relationships that broke more than my heart—they broke me. I wrongly sought safety in the arms of others, thinking that enough goodness on my part would finally earn me the right kind of love.

But here's the truth I found on the other side of heartbreak and confusion:

I wasn't looking for them.

I was looking for Him.

The One my soul and spirit were made for. I just didn't know it then.

And maybe… you've done the same.

If I could ask you one thing now, it would be this:

Feel that? That heartbeat?

It's proof. You're here on purpose. Your story isn't over.

It's the sound of survival. The rhythm of redemption. That devine echo of a God who never left your side, even when you were curled in the dark, whispering prayers that seemed to shatter on the ceiling.

But you're still here.

You made it.

Maybe not without scars or detours or nights you wish you could erase.

But still—you're here. And that alone is a miracle.

This book was never about them—the ones who hurt me, left me, or made me feel invisible. It was never about blame. It was always about helping you find Him.

The real Him.

Not the one we thought we'd find in a man's attention, affection, or validation.

Not the God-shaped hole we tried to fill with adrenaline, addiction, attachment or approval.

But Him—the One who formed you in the womb.

Who counted every tear.

Who waited patiently while you searched in all the wrong places so

LOOKING FOR HIM IN ALL OF THEM

that when you finally turned around, you'd realise... He was always right there.

I thought I was looking for love. But I was looking for Him.

I thought I needed rescuing.

But the Rescuer had already written my name on His palm.

And perhaps, without even knowing it, your heart was searching for Him too!

So now, on these last pages, please don't forget:

You were never too broken. Never too far gone.

Never too much—or not enough—or too late.

You've always been the one He loves unconditionally.

This isn't the end of your story—rather the beginning of a new chapter.

The one where you stop chasing love that costs your peace.

Where you stop watering dead ideals out of fear of being alone.

Where you finally turn your gaze to the only One worthy of your whole heart.

You are not crazy.

You are not weak for loving deeply.

You are not even foolish for hoping.

You are healing.

You are rising.

You are beginning again—not because you failed, but because you are favoured.

You're stepping out—out of the shadows, out of shame, out of survival-mode and into the glorious light of who God created you to be: Whole, radiant, bold and deeply loved.

Not because someone finally saw your worth.

But because He did.

Right there in the quiet centre of your soul—in the unwavering presence of the One who calls you Beloved.

So before we close this book please hear this:

You are not alone.

You are not forgotten.

You are not behind.

You are becoming.

Becoming whole. Becoming strong. Becoming wise.

You are becoming who you were always created to be.

And when love comes again—because it will—you won't know it by chaos or butterflies.

You'll know it by peace. By the quiet confirmation of the Spirit within—the one that no longer needs convincing you are worthy.

Because now… you know what genuine love looks like.

It looks like Jesus.

So, from one heart to another:

LOOKING FOR HIM IN ALL OF THEM

Lift your head.

Dry your tears.

Open your hands.

He's been here all along.

You're not searching for Him in them anymore.

You've found Him.

And maybe the most beautiful part? He never stopped looking for you.

> "My beloved spoke and said to me, 'Arise, my darling, my beautiful one, come away with me. For now the winter is past, the rain has ended and gone. The flowers are blooming all over the earth. The time of singing has come, and the voice of the turtle dove can be heard in our land. The fig tree forms its early fruit, and the blossoming vines spread their fragrance. Arise, my darling, my beautiful one, come away with me!'"
> *Song of Solomon 2:10-12 TPT*

> "To provide for those who grieve—to give them a crown of beauty for ashes, the oil of joy instead of mourning, the garment of praise instead of a spirit of despair.
> *Isaiah 61:3 (TPT)*

A Gift to Guide Your Journey

Your story isn't over. If something stirred in you as you read these pages, may I invite you to take the next step.

Download your free 7-Day Reflective Journal and begin your own journey of healing, hope, and wholeness. I truly hope it supports you and brings clarity to your journey.

Visit: simone.cassell.com/resources

With love,
Simone Alysha Cassell

An Invitation

If something stirred in your heart and you're ready to say yes to Jesus, you can start with this:

Jesus, I need You.
I believe You are the Son of God.
Thank You for loving me, for dying for me, and for
giving me new life. I open my heart to You. Please
forgive me, make me new, and help me follow You.
Amen.

If you prayed that prayer—welcome home. I encourage you to find a Bible-believing church or community where you can grow, be supported and discover more of who God created you to be.

Here's what I've learned through it all: Don't give up; don't be impatient; be entwined as one with the Lord. Be brave and courageous, and never lose hope. Yes, keep on waiting—for He will never disappoint you!
Psalm 27:14 TPT

ABOUT THE AUTHOR

Simone Alysha Cassell is an author, speaker and creative entrepreneur with a background in corporate sales, communications and brand positioning. She is Founder Director of several ventures, including her latest, Cassell Media Ventures (CMV)—a purpose-driven media company designed to amplify Kingdom-aligned stories through strategic representation and curated media partnerships. Simone's passion lies in amplifying faith-driven media to bridge faith, creativity, and culture.

Simone founded Scribes & Scepter Publishers, the sister company within Cassell Media Ventures, dedicated to empowering authors and storytellers with a platform to share transformative narratives that align with Kingdom values. Through this venture Simone hopes to build bridges between impactful voices and the media world, ensuring stories that inspire and transform reach audiences who need them most.

Simone resides on the Gold Coast, Queensland, Australia.

www.ingramcontent.com/pod-product-compliance
Lightning Source LLC
Chambersburg PA
CBHW020540080526
44583CB00013B/928